Rights of the Heart

Rights

of

the

Heart

Pat Maximoff

Also by Pat Maximoff

Occupation Upside Down
Going to Nias

Rights of the Heart

✦

A Wisconsin North Woods Heritage

Pat Maximoff

iUniverse, Inc.
New York Lincoln Shanghai

Rights of the Heart
A Wisconsin North Woods Heritage

iUniverse books may be ordered through booksellers or by contacting:

iUniverse
2021 Pine Lake Road, Suite 100
Lincoln, NE 68512
www.iuniverse.com
1-800-Authors (1-800-288-4677)

Photograph: Bob Maximoff
Sketches and cover design: Pat Maximoff

ISBN-13: 978-0-595-38627-7 (pbk)
ISBN-13: 978-0-595-83007-7 (ebk)
ISBN-10: 0-595-38627-X (pbk)
ISBN-10: 0-595-83007-2 (ebk)

Printed in the United States of America

For

All the people who have come to our cottage

and

All the people we wish had come to our cottage

and

All the people who have cottages of their own

Apology

Most of these stories are completely true, but not all. I did not carry a camera through the past. In some cases where memories have hazed, I have edited, condensed, and enlarged. I have gathered glimpses of several characters into a single person. I have changed names to protect the guilty. I have filled out missing pieces with probabilities. I have done my best to write emotional truth.

Contents

Acknowledgments

Thanks to my sister, Marjorie, and my husband, Bob, for sharing their memories and their skills; to Dr. Mary Bentzen and Sharlyn and John Heron for editorial support; to the members of the Northern Wisconsin String Ensemble for liking what I write; and to Dave and Miriam Karll for holding it all together.

The Cottage

1

The Cottage

We're installing air conditioning!

Air conditioning?

The cottage isn't insulated. You can't even live here in the wintertime. It goes down to forty below zero in northern Wisconsin.

But Bob insists on air conditioning. He says we need it because we're getting older, I'm a heart patient, and it's ninety-four degrees outside.

I admit that I don't feel good. The drive from California was a nightmare, close to one hundred degrees in Nevada and Wyoming. I'd promised the doctor that I'd get out and walk every two hours, but when I did, I got breathless and giddy.

We arrived here late Friday. It was hotter in Eagle River than I've ever known it to be. Even the cottage, usually ten degrees cooler than town, was stifling. We slept with a fan on, lying splayed over the bed so our perspiring bodies would catch every breeze.

On Sunday, I felt dizzy and noticed I was down to two nitroglycerin tablets.

Sunday!…When doctors don't work, and pharmacies are closed.

I thought we might get nitroglycerin at the Eagle River Hospital. On the way, I pulled out the paper that gives my medical history, my medications, and my insurance information.

The hospital air conditioning felt heavenly!

The doctor looked at my paper, the nurse took my blood pressure, and they wouldn't let me out.

At least, it was cool!

The doctor knows a man in Three Lakes who installs air conditioners. He's going to install one in our cottage on Thursday.

Grandfather must be turning over in his grave.

◆   ◆   ◆

Grandfather built this cottage, Grandfather and an Indian carpenter. They built it and stained it dark brown to match the woods.

I never knew my grandfather. He died before I was born, but Mother talked about him often. When she did, her voice went low and mysterious, like when she talked about art or sex or God.

According to Mother, Grandfather was a genius. He was an archaeologist, a professor, and Chaplain of Northwestern University. He knew six living languages and four dead ones. He did stand-up comedy, and he played the violin. He must have been an OK carpenter, too, because here is the cottage, still standing after almost a century. Of course, we've given it a bit of help from time to time.

Grandmother and Grandfather met in Evanston, Illinois, and were married in Grandfather's church. They moved into an old Victorian house on faculty row and had two girls, first Emma and then Mother.

Every four years, Grandfather got a year of sabbatical leave and went into his archaeologist mode. He deposited his wife and daughters in Europe and set off to dig things up in the Middle East. Mother and Emma had to fend for themselves in foreign schools. By the time they were in their teens, both girls were comfortable on two continents and fluent in French, Italian, and German.

Mother was a good student, but Emma was a paragon, head of her class, popular, and beautiful. I've seen pictures of her. She had perfect features. Mother's jaw was too square, her black eyebrows too straight, and her blue eyes too deep-set for beauty.

In 1908, Emma was selected valedictorian of her class, Mother was finishing high school, and life was blooming. There were parties, concerts, excursions, and there was always music. Mother played the piano, Emma sang, and my grandparents glowed with pride.

Then Emma came down with pneumonia. A week later, she was dead.

They closed the university so that her schoolmates could accompany her casket from the old Victorian house to the church where her parents had married and wed.

Small solace.

People say that the most excruciating sorrow you can have is from the death of a child.

Grandfather took the family to Italy to get away, but there were memories there, too, so they returned to Evanston.

Grandfather began taking long fishing trips in the North Woods.

A couple of years later, he bought this land and built this cottage. It is on a forested hill, between two lakes, and is protected by several acres of woods, a new place for new memories, with room for joy.

◆   ◆   ◆

I'm sitting at my laptop computer in the original room of the cottage Grandfather built.

This room is about eighteen by twenty-four feet, with a peaked roof above walls about eight feet high. The roof joists and beams are exposed. There is a fireplace at one end of the room, and an old pump organ at the other.

The fireplace is faced with stones. Among them, I'm told, are stones that Grandfather brought back from "The Holy Land." The rest are pure Wisconsin, rounded and smoothed by the mountains of ice that rolled them here in glacial times.

For years, the fireplace was our only heat. It draws beautifully if you set the fire back far enough. Its only fault is that Grandfather forgot to put in a damper.

On the mantle, are two oil lamps, the kind with circular wicks and heavy glass shades. They were brought up here when the Evanston house was wired for electricity. For many years, kerosene lamps were the only lights we had. We cooked on a kerosene stove.

We originally had two wire-and-frame studio couches, one on each side of the organ. They made a lot of sleeping space, but mice got to the mattresses. Now we have innerspring mattresses with proper spreads and lots of pillows. We threw the old frames into the swamp.

We've kept the old box couch beside the fireplace.

You'd never know to look at it, but the top of that couch swings open, and the base is one big, wooden box. We used to store our bed linens and quilts and towels there to protect them from the small creatures who are our winter tenants. Now we use it for things we don't know what to do with but can't bear to throw away: lace-edged linens too fragile to use, a couple of fishing rods, our sons' old BB gun, a couple of stained pillows I intend to cover some day, and a quilted bag into which you're supposed to zip yourself in order to keep warm when you're sitting down. It is designed to leave arms free, and seems like a good idea until you need to stand up. There is one of Grandmother's hats. That hat, a black straw muffin with a veil, was probably the height of fashion in 1901; Old Queen Mary wore hats like that. I know it's a genuine antique, but unfortunately, it has been sat on.

There are two rocking chairs and a low table in front of the fireplace, and a kitchen table in the middle of the room.

I'm uncertain as to what is called a kitchen table these days, but when I was growing up, a kitchen table was a plain wooden table about thirty inches high, with a two-by-three foot top, four doweled legs, and a missing drawer. We have two of them, one in the living room and one on the back porch. Each is covered with oilcloth and has its complement of four straight, wooden chairs. All of the chairs have tied-on chintz seat covers. The ones in the living room hide the composition seat covers that we thumb-tacked on during the Depression when the original wicker seats gave out.

The pine-planked floor is dark from years of swabbing with tung oil.

The dirt road that ran through our property in my childhood has been widened and leveled and paved. The grading has cut dangerously into our hill, which is eroding at an alarming rate. Snowplows and runoff from the spring melt have cut away at the other side as well. The cottage, which used to rest on a rounded summit, now sits on a kind of cone, like a hat on a slope-shouldered man.

Year-round houses nudge our property lines on the ends of both stretches of shoreline.

We've been assigned a proper street address.

Why do we keep the place, what with the taxes and the upkeep and growing urbanization? It's obviously too expensive for us. The cottage is bound to fall down one of these days. Air-conditioning, indeed! We live in California, for Pete's sake! Why don't we just rent a place in Tahoe? How about the national parks?

Maybe it's because here we can pick our own wild flowers.

Maybe it's because we have our own wandering room.

Maybe it's because we're crazy.

The Trip

2

The Trip

We're going to put the air conditioner high up under the eave on the left side of the front wall. It seems the most inconspicuous place, not where you'd normally look.

There are lots of other things in the room to look at—beds loaded with colored cushions and a Plains Indian mandala shield that Bob and I bought when our car broke down in Utah.

Hanging from a rafter is a long piece of driftwood, carved by ice and water into sweeping lines and curves and hollows. Our son, Tim, found it in the lake, pulled it out, cleaned and polished it, and freed its beauty.

On the far wall above the organ is a brightly painted wooden plate. I don't know where it came from, but it's pretty.

And there's the pump organ itself. The case is gracefully carved walnut, with crimson cloth showing through fretwork on each side of the music rack. It was a wedding gift to my grandparents. It still works.

There is a lot to distract attention, but how inconspicuous can a 9,000 BTU air conditioner be?

Bob warns me that it may be noisy.

I try to reconcile noise with the memory of my mother sitting at the organ, her face bright with the golden light of sunset through the window. She is playing a hymn, "Day Is Dying in the West," and we children are singing. The organ, our voices, and the wind in the trees are the only sounds.

◆   ◆   ◆

People warned Mother that if she married a man a quarter-century her senior, she'd be left a widow, perhaps with children, and then what would she do? Thank goodness she didn't listen! Daddy died at age ninety-six, and Mother died four months later.

Daddy was a big, gentle man, the son of Scandinavian immigrants. He was a minister like Grandfather, but Daddy got his call to the ministry while walking through a cornfield. No matter how much Mother brushed him off, polished him up, picked out his suits, and corrected his table manners, he retained a whiff of the Kansas prairie.

Mother and Daddy honeymooned at the cottage.

They brought Grandmother along.

According to Mother, they had set off in Daddy's car and got about as far as Wilmette, when Mother started worrying about how Grandmother was coping with the departure of her only remaining child. Mother asked Daddy to turn around and go back and see if Grandmother would like to come along. Surprisingly, he did. Even more surprisingly, Grandmother accepted.

Mother didn't see anything strange about this. It just goes to show that there can be great cultural differences between generations.

There was another structure on the property then, a World War I camp tent that Grandfather had bought from army surplus. You used to see a lot of those tents in places like Scout camps and CCC housing. They consisted of heavy canvas stretched over a collapsible wooden frame that was mounted on a platform. Our tent was in a clearing in the woods, far enough away from the cottage for privacy. A third path led to the privy.

I assume that my parents used the cottage, and Grandmother got the tent. I can't be sure.

Grandmother died just before the Great Depression came along. All of Grandmother's savings were in the stock market, so Mother lost everything she had inherited, except real estate. Daddy didn't have anything in the first place.

At that time, Daddy was managing the Methodist Book Concern, which distributed printed materials to churches throughout a four-state area. In order to balance the books without firing anybody, Daddy and his staff all took salary cuts.

I remember sitting at the dinner table listening to a discussion about whether my parents could afford to keep a car. Turned out Daddy had to have one because, although he took the streetcar to work, he needed a car to get to the country churches where he preached for free because they couldn't afford ministers of their own.

Mother set about making real estate pay.

She divided the old Evanston house into rooms and suites that she rented out to graduate students and faculty retirees.

She rented out our Kansas City home for the summers. We would store our good dishes and silver in the attic, and Daddy, who couldn't afford a long vacation, took a room near his office so strangers could live in our house.

Mother rented out the cottage during June. She said the rent paid the taxes. We didn't have a place to live for a month, but Mother had that figured out, too. Oil companies, a favored investment for retired professors, couldn't pay dividends during the Depression and issued gasoline coupons instead. Mother accepted gas coupons instead of rent, and in June we took to the road with a tent on our running board.

We saw a lot of the country during June, and always ended up in Evanston where Mother always found us a place to stay. A graduate student had completed his studies. A retiree was on vacation. The professor downstairs was on sabbatical.

When July came, the renters went home, and the cottage was ours.

Daddy had a clergyman's pass to ride the train. He traveled free from Kansas City to Chicago and caught the El to Evanston, so we could all go up to the cottage together.

We started early in the morning with our Oakland sedan crammed for the journey. Our auto trunk was strapped to the back, our suitcases tied on top, our ice chest, stocked with sandwiches and potato salad, on one running board, and the tent on the other in case we had to stop somewhere. You never knew how much car trouble to expect.

We'd packed the car the night before because packing took time and ingenuity. It was a three-dimensional jigsaw puzzle. You had to get everything inside that you couldn't put outside. There were things that would be handy at the cottage: old furniture or kitchen utensils, things to eat en route, water, pillows, a game or two, a violin, a ukulele, and last-minute items that you almost forgot. You had to leave some room for passengers, and everything was tied down because, unless it rained, you kept the windows open, and things could blow away.

We started out with Daddy in the driver's seat, Mother beside him, and we children in back, but we changed around along the way. Sometimes Mother drove while Daddy slept, and we kids could be anywhere.

With luck, the trip only took a day.

We picked up Highway 45 west of Winnetka, rode through country up to the Wisconsin border. We inched and honked our way through Milwaukee traffic and entered rich, rolling Wisconsin farmland, where we kept a lookout for white horses. If you spotted a white horse and confirmed the fact by placing your thumb in your palm and then stamping it with your fist, you'd have good luck all day.

We ate our picnic lunch in Fond du Lac by Lake Winnebago.

Highway 45 was a two-lane road, mostly concrete or asphalt, but sometimes gravel and occasionally dirt. You could get stuck behind a horse-drawn farm wagon or a tractor. We sang songs, found pictures in the clouds, fought, and napped.

Oshkosh was a high point because, aside from making "OshKosh B'Gosh" overalls, Oshkosh was a lumber town. Logs floated down the river to the timber mills, and if you were lucky, there might be a logjam, and you could look down from the bridge and see men walking the logs, spinning them under their feet to clear the way.

After clearing Tigerton, we began calling off the names of the towns we went through, Wittenberg, Eland, and Birnamwood. All the towns had speed limits of fifteen miles an hour, so you had time to wonder what it would be like to live there. Old houses set back from the road, white churches with steeples and bells, green and shaded town squares, courthouses with memorial statues or maybe a World War I artillery piece. When we stopped for gasoline, the

attendant pumped it by hand. He and Daddy talked about important things: politics, the weather, the corn crop; while I watched
pink-tinged gasoline bubble and swirl in the calibrated glass cylinder at the top of the pump.

If all went well, if we didn't have a flat tire or run into rain or skid
off a muddy section and have to be pulled out by a team of horses,
we made Antigo by late afternoon.

Fewer farms. More trees. Fresher air. You could smell pines and
water. A thrill of excitement! We were getting close!

Daddy looked at his watch and at the angle of the sun. We had to
get to the Clearwater store before it closed!

For years, I thought the town of Clearwater was just the general
store because I couldn't see any houses. They were all hidden back
in the woods. The store stood by the road, all by itself, a rectangular
frame building with three plank steps leading to a stoop and a screen
door. You could buy groceries, milk, eggs, bread, meat, and home-
grown vegetables. You could buy kerosene for your lamps, and lamp
chimneys and wicks. There were fishing rods and nets and bait pails.
I liked the fishing lures, so pretty with feathers and glittering metal,
but Daddy never bought any. He said a bit of bacon worked just as
well. There were always flies buzzing about, and strips of flypaper
hanging from the ceiling. And there was a slot machine.

Slot machines were evil. People played them and couldn't stop,
and lost all their money and their homes, and their wives and children starved.

I knew this, but I still yearned to play that slot machine.

Our parents stocked up for the cottage, while we children poked
around and picked up things we wanted, and were told, "No."

"Here, fill this." Mother handed me the large thermos.

"Say, 'please'."

She smiled. Her voice softened. "Of course! Please."

I took the thermos outside to the hand pump, and hung it, mouth open, on the faucet. I grasped the hard metal handle. Several pushes with both hands, a warning gurgle, and fresh well water gushed out. We always brought extra water for our first night because sometimes the gasoline pump down in the boathouse didn't want to be bothered.

It might be twilight by the time we turned off Highway 45 onto the county road. Ungraded and unpaved, the road rose and fell with the rolling contour of the earth. The woods wrapped around us like a blanket.

We watched for familiar landmarks in the growing darkness.

At last Daddy braked and changed into low gear. The car growled onto the ruts of our driveway and bumped and lurched up our hill.

The cottage stood dark and still under the trees.

We got out of the car. A jingle of keys, and Daddy unlocked the door, pushed it open. We entered dim emptiness and waited, smelling mothballs and must.

The scratch of a match, a flame, and the warm, golden glow of a kerosene lamp. The room came to life, the organ, the fireplace, the beds, the chairs. There, on the mantle, was the glass of feathers I'd saved last year, my sister's box of watercolors on the game shelf.

"I'm going down to the lake!"

"Not now. I need you to bring things in. We've got to make the beds. It's suppertime. You can go down in the morning."

"In a minute."

Through the kitchen, through the back door, onto the porch, and stopped. Far below, calling me, silver water shimmered through black silhouettes of leaves.

"Tomorrow."

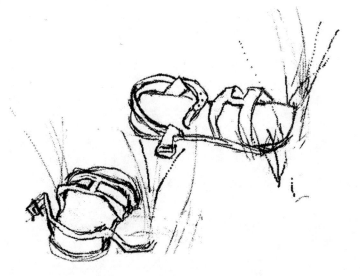

Children

and the Woods

3

Children and the Woods

Mother tried to make us wear shoes in the woods, but it was a lost cause. You couldn't walk like an Indian in shoes. As soon as we were out of sight of the cottage, the shoes came off. The soles of my feet became as calloused as leather.

"We" meant me and any children I was with at the time. This obviously did not include my sister, Marjorie, who was six years older than I, which made her more than a child. She was not an adult, either, but lived in a special realm of which I was not yet a citizen.

"We" might mean me and Elizabeth Snyder, who lived down the road on the Meta Lake side where her parents rented cottages in the summer, or "we" could be me and visiting children of my parents' friends.

"We" was most likely to mean me and one or more of Harry's children.

Harry was my father's son by his first wife. He was my half-brother, but he was almost as old as Mother. He was a combat veteran of both World War I and of alcoholism, and he had four children.

When Harry's wife died in childbirth, the new baby, Billy, came to live with us. My parents offered to take the other children as well, but Harry couldn't admit his failings as a father. He had commanded men, he said, and certainly he could handle his own family. According to his children, he ran his household like a boot camp and backed his authority with a razor strap.

In the summertime, Harry allowed his children to spend time at the cottage.

Sturdy, self-sufficient Howard was three years older than I, and pretty Julie was older by a year. Dark, intense Norman had been a toddler when his mother died and lived in a desperate little world of his own. Youngest of all, was our Billy.

It was hard to explain our relationship, so if anybody asked us, we said we were cousins.

Except for Julie and me.

We told everybody we were twins.

We didn't look alike. Julie had big brown eyes. Mine were pale and blue. Her hair was chestnut and wavy. Mine was blond and straight. She had nicely rounded arms and legs. I was skinny. But I wasn't jealous. Of course not. You have to be loyal to your twin.

One summer, Julie and I decided to prove our twinship by speaking in unison. We got pretty good at it, but we couldn't do it very fast. If you wanted a quick answer, you were out of luck. The boys thought we were funny. Mother's smile grew strained.

When Harry's children were at the cottage, the boys slept on cots in the tent, and everybody else except my parents slept in the big room. My parents slept in the bedroom. If there were extra people, Julie and I shared a couch. And each of us children had a share of an orange crate.

During the Depression, citrus fruit came in wooden crates that were about twelve by twelve by twenty-four inches. The sides were slats, but the ends were solid, and there was a solid divider in the middle. You could get them for free at any grocery store. You upended them, tacked oil cloth on top, made a little skirt by pleating fabric with thumb tacks, and you had a dressing table with two shelves, plenty of room for shorts, shirts, underwear and a tooth brush.

There was always something to be done at the cottage. Dishes to wash. Floors to sweep. Garbage to be taken out and buried in the woods. Lamp chimneys to be cleaned, and wicks to be trimmed. Beds to be made.

"No? You're on vacation? That's too bad. You have to make your bed because other people are using the room, too."

"Ha! Ha! Your turn to sweep the outhouse!"

Harry had a series of housekeepers, but there was only one that stayed very long. Her name was Mrs. Smith. Mrs. Smith was the only one Mother trusted enough to ask her to take charge one summer while Mother escaped for a vacation with Daddy. I liked Mrs. Smith. So did Julie. So did the boys. Mrs. Smith hugged children.

Mrs. Smith didn't come up the next summer. I heard Mother tell somebody that Mrs. Smith had thought she could reform Harry, marry him, and give the kids a real mother. It didn't work out.

We children had the run of the woods. We knew better than to go into the swamps or eat blueberries without crowns. We knew how to search under the leaves for sweet, wild strawberries, and we knew that if you encountered a bear, you should move very slowly. We knew how to take off leeches with salt. We knew we had to be back before sunset.

I know now that the trails we followed were deer trails, but then we imagined them as paths left over from Indian days. We made bows and arrows out of branches and string. They didn't work very well.

We made a swing out of an inner tube and some rope.

Howard, who knew everything, showed us how to make a slingshot out of a forked branch, the leather tongue of a shoe, and strips of inner tube. We had slingshot competitions. When we were tired of that, we just shot stones into the trees to hear them rustle through the leaves and fall onto the leaf-mulched forest floor.

Once, Julie shot a stone and, instead of just a rustle, there was a sharp cry and a thud as a small body fell to the ground. It was a chipmunk, and it had been shot in the eye. Julie started to cry. I picked up the poor little thing. It was soft and warm and limp. We carried it back to the cottage and laid it on the kitchen table. Everybody gathered around, sharing sympathy and suggestions. We felt a faint heartbeat. Mother found a little box and a scrap of old towel. Gently, she washed the wound. One eye was shut and appeared to be all right. The other eye protruded. It looked as though it could fall right out.

We waited.

The chipmunk stirred and made a small sound.

"Ah-h-h!"

Miraculously, the little animal recovered, except for his bad eye that stuck out and turned white. We named him "Popeye" and fed him nuts and bits of bread. When he seemed well enough, we let him out into the woods. He scampered off, but the next day he was back, sitting up on his hind legs, his little front paws hanging, his one eye bright. He came up and ate his pieces of bread right from our hands. You could feel his soft nibble tickling your palm.

"I think he likes us," whispered Julie.

"Yeah."

"I guess he didn't see what hit him."

"Yeah."

"I just hope he never finds out."

I guess he never did because he was back the next year, and the year after. Then he was gone.

A porcupine lived under our cottage for several years. We walked softly when it was near because someone, Norman I think, said that a porcupine could shoot its quills.

Mother said that was nonsense, but one couldn't be too careful.

Sometimes, deer came right up to the cottage. We would hold out food, motionless so as not to startle. Still. Breathless. So beautiful. So big. Large dark eyes questioning if we were friendly. And... sometimes...a dignified step, another, a bend of the lovely head, and our offerings were accepted.

We swam in Meta Lake because, being a spring lake, it was clearer than Catfish Lake, and calm. Catfish had a lot of algae in it, particularly after Roosevelt's Civilian Conservation Corps built a dam two lakes up the chain. They put in a boatlift, too, so people could still boat the chain, but that didn't keep the lakes clear. People said that at least algae should help the fishing. Fish like algae, don't they?

We didn't have a dock on Meta Lake, but you could always find a log to float on. There were water wings for the timid.

"How long can you stay under?"

"Longer than you can."

"Watch my breaststroke." Chin held high so as not to get water up the nose.

"You look like a frog."

Back up the hill, where feet had to be washed off on the back porch before you could go into the house.

We had a rowboat. It was named the *William Alice* after Billy and a friend of Marjorie's who came up one year. We kept our rowboat in the pump house down on Catfish.

Every year, before it could be used, the boat had to be pulled out, turned over, scraped and caulked, and sunk in the lake for a day or two so the water would swell the wood and seal the seams. Then it was brought ashore again and allowed to dry enough to paint.

Rowing that boat was an art because we didn't have modern oar-locks. Our oarlocks had a flange that kept the oars from sliding through, but there was no little rod to hold them in a horizontal position. You had to do that for yourself. This had its advantages. You could turn the oars perpendicular to the water when you wanted speed, and feather them on the exit so there would be no drag.

I didn't know what a modern oarlock was until I saw one on one of Elizabeth Snyder's father's boats. We didn't get modern oarlocks until I was in high school. I didn't like them at first. Where's the challenge when the locks do it for you?

We didn't carry life preservers, either, but before any of us were allowed to use the boat by ourselves, we had to prove that we could get to shore from any part of the lake.

Catfish Lake has three parts, each of which would make a good-sized lake of its own. To pass the family aquatic safety test, you had to go out into the middle of any of these parts, get into the water somehow, (you were usually pushed) and make your way to shore. It didn't matter how you did it. All you had to do was get there alive.

The secret, of course, was that you didn't have to swim at all if you didn't want to. You could just lie on your back and kick. That's what I did.

Howard was the first of Harry's children to pass the test. He actually swam. I don't know where he learned how. Howard had ways of picking up skills and information independent of his family. He did a fairly presentable freestyle and only stopped a few times to tread water. He climbed out of the water, breathless and triumphant. We were all impressed.

Norman was next, and he almost drowned. Scared-spitless dog paddle isn't a restful stroke. I remember pulling him into the boat. I don't remember his trying again, and, come to think of it, I don't remember that he ever took the boat out by himself.

I don't remember Billy's test, either, but he must have passed because he used the boat, and so did Julie.

The *William Alice* gave us another game. Who could row the fastest? We rowed singles and doubles and mixed sets. The judging was somewhat subjective, as we had no stopwatch and no other boat to row against. The rules could be a problem, too.

"No fair! Howard's in the back, and he's heavier than I am."

"O.K. We can balance that. Billy, move to the front."

"Hey! You're not supposed to stand up in a boat!"

"He's not standing, he's leaning."

"You're supposed to crouch."

◆　　　◆　　　◆

We were so young! Julie's eyes still sparkled with mischief, and Norman still could laugh. Now Billy is the only one of Harry's children still alive.

Howard joined the army and worked his way into West Point. He died a decade or so ago.

Julie tried to escape into marriage. After two children and a disastrous divorce, she spent the rest of her life battling the disease that killed her father.

Norman was his father's favorite child and greatest victim. After Harry died, Norman tried college, but it didn't take. He joined the army, but was discharged. He studied for the priesthood, but argued with his mentors and quit. Then he wandered around the country, doing a series of blue-collar jobs. He was in his twenties when he drove as far as he could go down the Florida Keys and shot himself.

Our Billy grew up to become a naval engineer. He followed his dream to the northwest and found waters and woods of his own.

◆   ◆   ◆

Where do children go today to dream their private dreams? Doesn't the pounding speed of living, with the flickering repetitions of the media, force them into a prison of other people's fantasies?

Maybe they like their prisons. People tend to like what they are used to. Maybe I'd like one, too, if I'd never known anything else.

But I have.

Down on the Catfish shore, there was a big rock nestled in the scarp, a few feet above the water. I found it by accident when I was in the woods following the deer trail that skirts the lake. I slipped and caught myself on the underbrush. When I looked down, I was standing on a rock. I looked back. The underbrush had closed above me, hiding the path. I looked out and saw the sweep of the lake. I sat there for a long time pretending that I was hiding.

The next time I was out in the boat, I looked along the shore for my rock. It took a while to find. It was well-camouflaged. Who would ever notice a little girl sitting on that rock?

I spent a lot of time on that rock. It was my secret place. I looked out on the lake and thought that if I stocked the *William Alice*, I could row down the chain to where it joined the Wisconsin River, and down the Wisconsin to the Mississippi, and down the Mississippi to the Gulf of Mexico, and from the Gulf of Mexico to the Atlantic Ocean.

Sometimes, I was allowed to take the boat out by myself after supper, when the sky was streaked with coral and rose, and the wind was down. I'd row and row, way out on the lake, pretending I was on my way to the sea. I'd row until it got dark and the tree-covered shoreline was black against the sky. I'd stop and look up at the sky and think of how far away the stars were. Then I'd pick up my oars and search along the silhouetted skyline for the tiny light I knew would be there. It was the only light in that whole black forest.

If there's only one light, it's like a star. You can see it for miles. My light was the oil lamp that Mother put in the cottage window to guide me home.

Technology

4

Technology

Why should I object to an air conditioner?

It's not as though we've never modernized anything before.

Our first great leap of technology took place during World War II. I was in that period between childhood and maturity when one is certain that one has graduated into real life, and childhood things like parents and history and a summer cottage are relegated to the box couch of triviality. I was in college.

Mother often used real estate as an excuse to visit me. We were having lunch when she told me she had installed electricity and plumbing in the cottage.

I put down my fork. "Oh?" I shrugged. Why should I care?

Mother hurried to explain that she hadn't thought we needed electricity and plumbing ourselves, but she could no longer rent a place with an outhouse.

"Nobody wants to rough it anymore."

"Mother, there's a war on. There's gas rationing." I don't know why that was relevant, but it seemed so at the time.

"I know, dear, but we still have to pay taxes." She leaned back and folded her hands. It was her signal for a discussion.

Mother liked to "discuss things." I wasn't fond of her discussions, but I knew when I was trapped. I gave my deepest, most meaningful sigh and resigned myself to the inevitable.

Where, I asked, was she putting the john?

"In the kitchen."

"In the kitchen?!"

She drew a diagram of what she'd done. It showed a rectangle on the living room side of the kitchen in which was outlined a commode, a sink, and a stall shower.

"What did you do with the kitchen table?"

"It's on the back porch."

"Oh."

No more wild blueberry pancakes to the cozy patter of rain on the kitchen roof.

"We have an electric stove."

No more friendly kerosene fumes.

"There are electric lights in all the rooms."

No more soft glow of kerosene lamps.

"And hot water."

No more cheerful singing of a boiling teakettle.

"And an electric water pump."

Eureka!

Did I mention that our cottage is on the top of a hill?

To get to Catfish Lake, you have to go down a long, steep path on steps that Grandfather carved out and faced with cut logs. Beside this path, about halfway down the hill and almost lost in the underbrush, is a sinkhole where an old well used to be. My grandparents hand-pumped their water from that original well when the cottage was first built. They carried the water in buckets up to the cottage where it was used for cooking and drinking and cleaning. Tooth brushing was done in the yard with the toothbrush in one hand, and a glass of water in the other. Baths were taken in the lake.

I guess water-hauling got to Grandfather because he installed his one modern appliance, a gasoline-powered water pump.

Down by the lake, there's a small shack which we call a boathouse because we store our rowboat there over the winter. It also houses our present well, which, I've been told, is so deep that it taps a spring below the level of the lake. Grandfather's water pump sat over this well, and a pipe ran from the boathouse all the way up the hill. In the old days, it ended at a faucet on the back porch. The faucet hung above a shelf containing two big, galvanized wash tubs with big, galvanized lids. You could swing the faucet over either tub, or allow the water to splash onto the floor. There were spaces between the floor planks. A child could stand under the porch and pretend it was raining.

About twice a week, someone had to go down to the boathouse and start the pump. First they had to prime it and swing the fly-wheel until it produced a big enough spark to fire up the engine. Finally, the engine would give a few loud coughs and, with a metallic chunking that could be heard for miles, started sucking up water and sending it up sixty-five feet to the house.

Meanwhile, you waited, listening, on the porch. First you heard a soft gurgling. It grew louder. The pipe trembled until, with a sputter and a gush, water poured out.

It was usually rust-colored. You had to hold the faucet over the floor until the water ran clear.

When the first tub was full, you swung the pipe over to the other tub. When it, too, was full, you swung the faucet over the shelf and yelled down to the boathouse.

"Hey."

A faint, "Hey!"

"OK!"

"OK!"

A moment, and the pump sputtered into silence.

Every week, you had to renew the water and wash out the tubs with baking soda before filling them again because water gets stale, and, even with the tops on the tubs, things get in, like bugs.

Yes, there was a lot to be said for an automatic electric water pump.

Mother's pump has given my engineering husband hours of diversion because, no matter what pump you have, you can't change the laws of physics. Sixty-five feet remains sixty-five feet, and water pressure remains a challenge. You can be in the middle of washing your hair, your head all over soap, when the water gurgles, fades to a trickle, and stops.

Bob has explained to me about pressure-height ratios, the weight of water, pipe sizes, storage and gravity, and all kinds of esoteric things. He's made a myriad of ingenious plans. He's talked of installing a big, industrial pump in the boathouse, or putting a second pump halfway up the hill. For years, he waited for that old pump to wear out so he could do something great and different.

The pump broke down while we were living overseas. My sister, Marjorie, was in the cottage at the time. She didn't want to bother us with a problem she thought we could do nothing about, so she searched around until she located a pump that was exactly like the old one. She was lucky, she told us because it was an old model, and they didn't make them any more.

I was proud of my husband. He turned bright red, but he mastered himself and thanked her.

Now we have a gauge in the bathroom. It reads the water pressure, so we know whether we can flush the john or do the dishes, or whether we should run the water pressure down until the automatic switch starts the pump down in the boathouse and it can build the pressure up again. That takes a while, but it's better than a flywheel.

◆   ◆   ◆

Rural electrification started during the Depression. It was a big thing, even through World War II. Our cottage was certainly rural.

We only went into town once a week to get the mail. Oh, yes, and to church on Sunday.

We ate a lot of ham and beans because ham keeps well, and dried beans last forever. We ate canned goods that Mother bought by the case from Montgomery Wards. We bought fresh food from a farm couple who lived about a mile down the road. They had cows and chickens and milk and butter and fresh vegetables. They also had Pomeranian puppies that I coveted, to no avail. Behind their frame house was a log dugout with a sod roof, which had been their first Wisconsin home. It served as root cellar, and as an icehouse for ice they had cut from the lake in the winter and kept cold under mounds of sawdust.

We didn't need their ice because we had a cooler.

When Grandfather added the kitchen, he dug into the hill beneath to make a storage room. He boarded its sides and dug a hole in the dirt floor, into which he put a metal-lined wooden box with a hinged cover. That was our cooler. It stayed cold, even in hot weather, just from the earth around it.

When the refrigerator came, the cooler went. Daddy was afraid it would rot, and someone might step through it and sprain an ankle.

Aside from that, the storage area hasn't changed much over the years. If you stand on the dirt floor and look up into the crawl space, you can still see the stumps of the trees that were cut to clear the area, and the hole that the old porcupine gnawed so he could get in and out during the winter.

The room has a big plank door, a very small, very dirty window, and is lit by a single bulb hanging from a rafter. Our water heater sits on cement blocks in the far corner. There are shelves with paint, stored lumber, rolls of roofing, and a footlocker. There are boxes of who-remembers-what, some fishing rods, and a minnow net. My old crib is there, too. We didn't use it for our own children because modern cribs are much handier, but its sturdy wooden ends and its screened top and sides make for convenient storage. Animals can't get in, and you can see what's in there.

A folded ladder leans against the side wall. There are tools, hammers, a shovel, a spade, and an axe. Farther in the shadows, hang a scythe and a two-man bucksaw. Nobody uses them any more.

The only time I saw anybody use that two-man bucksaw was when Daddy demonstrated it to Billy. They had a log on a trestle, and they worked, one on each side of the saw, alternately throwing their weight forward and back, push, pull, push, pull, deeper and deeper into the wood, until it surrendered and collapsed.

"That's the way we did it," said my father, proudly.

Billy wiped his perspiring face with his forearm and nodded.

Daddy used the scythe to cut the tall grass in the front yard. He swung it with an easy rhythm learned in his prairie childhood. You could tell he enjoyed it.

I was apprehensive when Bob taught the boys to use the axe.

"No problem," he said, "They'll be fine as long as they keep their eyes on where they want it to go."

Good advice.

Parents have been teaching their children how to use those ancient implements since before people built the cities Grandfather dug up.

No more. The swish of the scythe and the thwack of an axe have been replaced by the roar of lawnmowers and chainsaws.

I've considered fixing up that storeroom. It's always cool down there. If we'd finished that room, we might not need an air conditioner.

◆ ◆ ◆

Our most wrenching modernizations involved the media.

During my childhood winters, I was allowed fifteen minutes of radio a day. I had total freedom to choose what I wanted to hear, as long as it didn't break into Mother's symphony concerts or Daddy's news, and as long as I'd done my homework, my violin practicing, and whatever housework had been assigned me.

I usually chose Jimmy Allen, the Flying Ace, or Jack Armstrong, the All American Boy. Each ran for fifteen minutes. Programs for girls didn't exist.

We didn't have that problem at the cottage. No electricity, so we read books, played games, and roamed the woods.

Then the folks got a car with a radio.

I begged to be allowed my fifteen minutes. My parents refused. We didn't come to the woods to bring the world with us, they said. If I wanted stories, I could read, and if I wanted music, I could play my violin or the organ. I could not use the car radio. I might run down the battery.

Bob and I have been more lenient with our own children. We even bought a little radio for the cottage, but we only used it for news and the weather forecast. We pointed that out to the children. We told them how fortunate we were to have a special place where the outside world couldn't disturb us, a place where we could enjoy the beauty of nature, free of the drumbeats of the media. We didn't need outside entertainment.

The only time we brought in television for the children was during the 1976 Olympics. Our son, Tim, was into competitive swimming in Australia, and several of his teammates were on the Australian Olympic team. That seemed important enough to waive the rules. We rented a small black and white set. The reception was terrible. Too many trees.

Bob said we needed a better antenna.

We have drapes that can be pulled all across the front room to separate the sleeping couches from the rest of the room, so that children can go to bed while adults read and stay up. The drapes hang from a wire stretched beneath a rafter.

Bob touched the rabbit ears of the television to the wire. We got a hazy picture.

"It needs to be directional," Bob said, and left the room. We heard noises under the house. Bob reappeared with a strange sculpture made from pieces of pipe and twisted wire. He attached this creation to the rafter, then connected it to the drapery wire and the rabbit ears. The picture improved slightly.

Bob shook his head. Then he attached another wire to the sculpture and ran it out the window. We saw the summer Olympics through snow.

We returned the television the next day, but we rather liked Bob's sculpture. It hung around for a couple more years.

Both kids were grown and on their own when Bob had the accident that resulted in a detached retina. Now his vision is skewed. He can't read for any length of time, but he can watch television.

By that time, we had relocated to California, several days' drive from the cottage. We decided we needed something comfortable for the trip, something we could stand up in and sleep in, something with plumbing. We tried out an RV, but it was too big and awkward to drive. SUVs weren't yet in vogue, so we bought a panel truck. We had a bubble top put on it, and windows cut in the sides. We installed a hideaway back seat and a carpeted floor. Bob designed a water system with a sink and a tiny water pump that ran on a battery. We bought a battery-operated cooler, and we hid a port-o-potty under a little skirt. In a fit of terrible cleverness, we named our van "Vincent Van Go." Last, guiltily, we tucked a little ten-inch portable TV behind the back seat. We didn't tell the children.

The reception at the cottage was as terrible as before, but this time Bob was prepared. He'd learned how to make an antenna. He sat on the back porch of the cottage for several days, creating a gleaming metal tree with enough branches to detect every quiver of the ether. It even had a swivel so it could be turned and tuned to our hill. The pole that held it was slender, and the top fell sideways like a drooping flower, but Bob said that would be all right because he would fasten it to the chimney. He gave me the pole to hold while he carefully pushed his ladder into the sandy soil. Bob doesn't like ladders, particularly since developing his eye problem, but he refused to let me go up in his place. He braced himself against the stones of the base of the chimney and slowly rose, rung by cautious rung, until he could grab the edge of the roof. He held down a hand.

"Now?"

"Now"

I heard a mosquito humming near my neck.

"Careful!" said Bob, "You almost hit me!"

"Sorry."

The insect was inspecting my cheek.

"To your left a little."

Ouch!

"Did you say something?"

"No."

Bob rigged two straps around the chimney to secure the pole, then ran a connecting wire from the antenna through a tiny hole in the wall down near the baseboard. He tuned the antenna by turning the swivel outside, while I watched the screen inside and gave him cues. We got three and a-half stations! Of course, we had to take the whole thing down before we left and hide it under the house before the children turned up.

It was about three years later that Tim and Kristi said they wanted a phone in the cottage. They were really sorry. They knew how we felt about phones, but Kristi works for a tech firm, and she had to be able to work at the cottage. She needed a modem.

We had never had a phone at the cottage. We never needed a phone. We militantly did not want a phone. One of the great advantages of our cottage was its phonelessness. Years ago, when we came to the cottage on leave from overseas, the only person who knew how to reach Bob was his secretary in Kuala Lumpur, and she only had the phone number of our nearest neighbor, who was five minutes away by car, and fifteen minutes by foot. If there was an emergency, the neighbor could come over and tell us, and Bob could drive into town and return the call from the phone booth in front of the hardware store. When we came to the cottage, we left everything else behind. It was our magic place, our secret garden. If you wanted to reach us, you could write to us at "Maximoff, General Delivery," and if you wanted to see us, you were welcome to climb our hill.

We compromised a little when we began driving our van across country. The children worried that if we had any trouble, we wouldn't be able to get help, so we bought a cell phone. We never turned it on.

Now Kristi needed a modem.

We didn't want to be unreasonable. Things were changing. There was a telephone pole at the foot of our hill, and a gas line crossed part of our property.

And we weren't getting any younger.

Yes, we'd put in a phone, but in an unobtrusive place, under the mirror beside the door to the kitchen, where it is equally inconvenient to everything.

The children were suitably grateful.

Then Tim cleared his throat.

One more request.

It was embarrassing because they knew how we felt about change, and if we really hated the idea, they'd forget all about it.

The problem was that the reception had been terrible on the television they'd been renting every summer. Would we mind awfully if they put in cable?

Crime and the Cottage

5

Crime and the Cottage

On the wall in front of me is a large map showing "the chain" of twenty-seven connected lakes, with a myriad of spring lakes scattered among them. Our property lies between two of them, Catfish Lake, which is on the chain, and Meta Lake, which is self-contained.

Beneath the map, is a small bookcase into which I've put the atlas and a dictionary. My laptop could supply me with information about geography and lexicology, but I'm more comfortable with books. That's one of the good things about this place. It's well supplied with books.

On the cottage bookshelves, there are books that go back for decades, old books: *Uncle Tom's Cabin*, *Tales from the Crypt*, *The Magic Mountain*, and *Ten Nights in a Barroom*. There were two copies of *The Scarlet Letter* until I took one back to California. Crammed on a bookshelf beside the front door are *Living Age* magazines from the 1920s, with articles like "Anti-Semitism in Germany" and "Remaking Ruined France." There are articles by Andre Gide, Bertrand Russell, and a pathetically idealistic treatise entitled "Women and Bolshevism" by Leon Trotsky.

Another bookcase holds children's books from three generations: *The Cat in the Hat*, *Watership Down*, and a well-worn *Winnie-the-Pooh*.

First Latin Lessons, Revised, bears my sister's name on the flyleaf, with "In Case of Fire, Throw In!" added in pencil underneath.

There's Shakespeare, of course, and a Bible, and, in the kitchen, there is a copy of *The Boston Cooking-School Cookbook,* circa 1914.

People don't usually steal books.

They steal other things.

You can't help but wonder about people who break into your home. Why did they do it?

Sometimes, the reason is obvious. They want to steal things and sell them.

There used to be a secondhand store in what is now the parking lot behind DeByle's apparel store. You could find a lot of things you needed there, and for reasonable prices. You could get used refrigerators and stoves, old furniture, tools, pots and pans, and dishes. We bought our kitchen sink there. It was the neighborhood recycling center in the era before cast-offs and junk turned into antiques and collectibles. It's gone now, but before it closed, thieves stole our water pitchers, our basins, and even our chamber pots. We learned to hide things in the box couch, but some things are too big to hide. A lot of the furniture the folks lugged up from the Evanston house and the Kansas City house is gone.

But not all.

Some real over-a-hundred-year-old antiques are still here because, I suspect, nobody recognized them. Mother believed that children should be free to express themselves. One of the ways we expressed ourselves was by painting furniture. I remember sitting out on the grass with a brush and a can of enamel, happily painting a Victorian lady's rocking chair bright orange. Our pressed wood dining chairs have been royal blue, then maroon, and still later, chartreuse. The bureau in the bedroom is lavender; the lamp table, coral. The porch chairs are pink and baby blue, but worn places on the back reveal a varied history.

In recent years, I've removed several quarts of muddy enamel from two tea tables and a small bureau on the theory that, these days, conscientious thieves watch *Antiques Roadshow* and aren't interested in refinished furniture.

Not all intruders steal things. Our animal tenants leave us house gifts: mouse nests in unprotected upholstery or an organ full of acorns.

Some human trespassers don't take anything and leave no serious damage, just a broken lock or a jimmied window. Why do they do it? Are they just curious?

We figured out that one of our robbers was setting up house-keeping because he took two rocking chairs, a few dishes, some cooking utensils, and all of my spices.

In one winter of my childhood, somebody actually lived here. The fireplace had been used, our stores of wood and kerosene were depleted, and there were empty whiskey bottles on the porch. During Prohibition, too! Oh, my goodness! But the cottage had been swept. The linens had been washed, and every dish was clean!

In the nineteen-twenties and thirties, Mayor Kelly of Chicago and a friend of his (who everybody whispered was a gambler and a gangster) had summer places about two miles down the Catfish shore, on the other side of the entrance to the Cranberry Lake channel.

There weren't very many people on the lake then, no more than a couple of dozen, and most had small cottages or tourist cabins. Except, that is, for Mayor Kelly and his friend. Their houses were gigantic. So were their guesthouses and their boathouses. They even had electricity!

The gambler's mansion stood back in the trees, so you could only guess at its immensity. His boathouse was a Tudor masterpiece, two stories with stained glass windows on the second floor. When the door was open, you could see the three big powerboats that made huge wakes when they roared across the lake, full of sun-tanned passengers trailing laughter and scarves.

Mayor Kelly's three-story house was dark green with a parade of multi-paned windows with tall white shutters. His spacious lawn swept down to the shore where a life-sized painted statue of an Indian peered out over the lake.

Occasionally a seaplane roared into our lives, descending over our woods and sputtering to silence somewhere beyond. That meant the Kellys were having a party. We children would row all the way over there at night and sit in the boat, watching. It was like something out of F. Scott Fitzgerald. Music drifting from the house. Men in dinner jackets and women in long dresses strolling the lawn. You could see, through the tall windows, the silhouettes of dancers.

Just like the movies, only in color.

It was in one of those gangster years that someone broke into our cottage, made up our beds, left ashes in our fireplace and whiskey bottles on our porch.

We speculated in low, excited voices.

Everybody knew there were renegades in the woods: Al Capone, Baby Face Nelson, John Dillinger: bootleggers, fugitives from the FBI. Perhaps our visitors were henchmen of the gambler, felons who didn't dare stay in his house because it was too well-watched to be a safe hideaway. We couldn't know for sure, but wasn't it likely?

They must have cleaned up because they had enough enemies without adding us to their list.

I don't know what happened to Mayor Kelly. His place has changed hands several times. His friend next door left his whole place, boathouse and all, to the Catholic Church. They turned it into a retreat. Black-clad nuns strolled where flappers once frolicked. Someone told me that the game room behind the stained glass windows became a chapel.

◆   ◆   ◆

A few decades ago, Bob and I were again visited by a vandal. I've tried to imagine what was going through his mind.

There used to be an old player piano in the corner where I am sitting. The intruder poured sugar and flour all over the floor and took a hammer to the keyboard of the organ. He broke some of the keys and the little wooden hinges that open and close the stops. He left the organ case intact, but he ruined the piano. The case was splintered. The keyboard was in pieces. The player mechanism totally demolished. Even the strings were cut!

He must have hated piano lessons!

One tries to look on the bright side of things. Keeping a piano in an unheated cottage in the North Woods isn't a good idea. It was never in tune.

Bob spent the next summer carving new pieces for the organ. We didn't know what to do with the piano, so we left it. My sister came up later with her boys and dragged it down to the swamp.

People don't usually steal books. They destroy them.

The very first time someone broke into the cottage, I was six. I know I was six because it was the second summer after Grandmother died. I don't recall all the details but I have one mental picture.

It's clear as a snapshot.

Mother is standing by a broken window, her arms crossed over her chest, holding herself. Tears course down her cheeks. Around her, scattered all over the floor, lie the torn and water-stained remnants of her family Bible, the one with records back to colonial times.

Mother caught her breath in a sob.

"I brought it up here to be safe.

Land

Wars

6

Land Wars

The air conditioning man just called. The air conditioner hasn't arrived from Milwaukee, so he can't get it in until Thursday.

I don't know why the heat bothers me so much. My temperature controls seem to have aged along with the rest of me.

I shouldn't complain. Mother and Grandmother both lived here without air conditioning. On the other hand, both Mother and Grandmother died when they were six years younger than I am.

If they were here, they'd tell me to count my blessings.

O.K., I'll do that.

I'm grateful that I'm alive.

I'm grateful for modern medicine that has brought me to an age that Mother and Grandmother never reached.

I'm grateful that Bob and I are fairly well preserved. At least I think we are. It's hard to tell when people keep telling you how well you look, and you wonder why the subject came up.

I'm grateful to be here on the hill, instead of in town. It's always ten degrees hotter in town.

I'm grateful that when I do go into town, I can escape into an air-conditioned supermarket.

There are two immense supermarkets now, in a town that used to have one tiny general store. You can buy almost anything in Eagle River these days! Even live lobsters!

I think I'm grateful that I saw Jeff Snyder yesterday in Bonson's Supermarket.

I almost didn't recognize Jeff. He looked twisted, and his face was wrinkled, deep furrows of wrinkles like portly men get. But Jeff was no longer portly. He'd shrunk. We all have.

I don't think Jeff recognized me at first, but he talked politely until he put together the clues I fed him. I asked about his place on the lake. He said he'd had to sell it. His wife had a stroke and needs constant care.

He said his sister, Elizabeth, died last year.

When I remember how much time I spent playing with Elizabeth Snyder, I feel guilty that the thing I remember most about her is her appendicitis scar. She showed it to me in their outhouse. Bodily functions were more social then than now, and the Snyder outhouse was a three-holer. We were sitting side by side. Elizabeth was considerably overweight, and her rolling white stomach presented her scar brilliantly. I can see it to this day, shudderingly long, wide, and brilliant pink.

All the Snyders were overweight except Allan.

I had a crush on Allan. He was a year older than Elizabeth. He had dark hair and huge, blue eyes, and a quick, bright smile. He died a few years ago.

Jeff was a year older than Allan. He took after his mother, who had a slow, easy smile and looked like Eleanor Roosevelt.

Mr. Snyder had another son, Slim, by a former marriage. We didn't see Slim much. He weighed about three hundred pounds and lived his own life. He gained his fifteen minutes of fame about twenty years ago when he drove his car into a house. He died awhile back.

Their uncle, John Snyder, homesteaded forty acres between the lakes. He and Grandfather used to go fishing together. Grandfather bought this land from John Snyder.

When John Snyder died, his brother Melvin came up from Milwaukee and took over.

Mother seemed to think Grandfather's friendship with John and that long-ago transaction gave us a special relationship to the whole Snyder family.

I don't think Melvin Snyder shared Mother's feeling of obligation. He talked a lot about how he watched over our place and did favors for us, but, as I remember, he charged well for his labors, and it was his wife, Dora Snyder, who managed their place on the lake. Melvin spent most of his time running his electric business in town.

I have trouble being objective about Melvin Snyder. He still makes me mad.

The Snyders had six rental cottages on Meta Lake, as well as their summer house. There was a recreation building with a ping-pong table, an icehouse, a real sand beach with a permanent pier, and rowboats so the tourists could fish. They called it Wilderness Way. I was jealous of the tourist children whose parents rented cottages and who were treated with deference, while we only owned our land, and I was treated like an ordinary child.

The Snyders were the first people on Meta Lake to get electricity. Dora Snyder was not impressed. She preferred her old wood stove. She said it cooked better than any gas or electric stove ever invented. This angered her husband, who said it wasn't good for his business, but Dora Snyder paid him no heed. She just kept shoving in wood and moving her pans and skillets around to warmer or cooler parts of her big, black, cast iron range. She made pots of stew, and baked beans and cookies and cakes and her own bread. I ate a lot when I was at the Snyders.

One summer, we children discovered a lucrative little business. We caught grasshoppers in the cleared field across the road from Wilderness Way, and sold them to Snyder's renters for bait. Unfortunately, Melvin Snyder found out, which, come to think of it, wasn't hard. Who could help noticing a bunch of children spending hours leap-frogging around in a field? Anyhow, Mr. Snyder told Mother that we had to stop chasing grasshoppers. It wasn't that he disapproved of honest enterprise. It was that the grasshoppers were his grasshoppers. His children could catch them, but no outsiders.

I never felt quite welcome at Snyder's again.

Then there was the matter of the landfill.

In the Depression, a lot of lakeshore owners found themselves land-poor. They wanted to sell land, but most of the Meta shore was cranberry bog. In order to attract buyers, they needed to "improve" their shorelines. One of the easiest ways was to use a machine that, for lack of a better name, I'll call a sand-sucker. It sucked sand up from the lake bottom and blew it onto shore. You could turn a messy cranberry bog into a nice beach with a sand-sucker.

Melvin rented himself a sand-sucker and got the beach-making monopoly on Meta Lake. Mother contracted for a hundred feet. Melvin filled fifty.

Mother said he'd probably misunderstood.

And there were the fir trees.

These days, when you look at the beautiful evergreens around Vilas County, it's hard to believe that the original evergreens were all but eliminated in the lumber boom of the 1880s.

In the 1930s, Melvin offered to plant some baby firs on our land. He said he was putting a couple of hundred seedlings in the field where we'd caught our grasshoppers, and he'd have a few left over. Did we want them? He'd give us a good price. Mother was delighted. It wasn't until some time later that Daddy ran across an article about the federal reforestation plan, and Mother realized that Melvin had charged her for trees he'd got for free.

Mother used to say how fortunate we were that Melvin Snyder treated our place as if it were his own. It was years before she realized that, to Melvin, it was. Melvin never believed that when you sell something, it stops being yours.

There is an old trail that borders our Meta shore. It runs from the county road down to the lake, goes along the shore for several hundred feet, then turns and meets the county road across from our driveway. Melvin Snyder still owned the property beyond ours. The only way he could get to the his lake shore through his own property was by a trail farther up the county road. Our trail was more convenient, so we told him he was welcome to use it.

We didn't tell him he could sell it.

But he did.

We found out when we came up one summer to find our little trail had been widened and graveled, and was sporting a mailbox.

We followed the trail past our property line for quite a way into Melvin's property where we found a man building a house. We introduced ourselves. The man was a high school teacher from Illinois. He welcomed us to his new house and introduced us to his family. He said he'd always wanted a house on a lake, and now he was building one.

We admired his house, then asked him if he knew he was driving through our land.

His jaw dropped. Melvin Snyder had told him the trail was public property.

Bob and I looked at each other. Was it worth making a fuss? Did we want to spend our money and vacation time in court? Summer people were always at a disadvantage because hearings tend to be scheduled in the winter. And it wasn't the schoolteacher's fault.

We decided to give our new neighbor a limited right of way.

Melvin Snyder was conveniently out of town.

◆   ◆   ◆

Then came Melvin's proposed land swap.

Melvin wanted, he said, to build a new house for Dora. It would be just his side of our property line, where his wife would have a beautiful view of the lake and could watch the changing seasons and the birds and all. But to keep things simple, he'd like to straighten the property lines a little. The original lines were based on government surveys that went due north and south. The shorelines of the lakes were on a slant. It didn't make sense. So how about a trade? He'd straighten out his line between the shore and the old road and, in exchange, he'd straighten out our property lines on the Catfish side. He'd even pay for the survey.

According to Mother, Melvin was pointing to a nice little piece of land between the logging trail and the Meta shore, land that Mother would be happy to part with to please an old friend.

When the survey came, Melvin had claimed almost a third of our Meta property. In exchange, we would get a small, inaccessible triangle of his land across the road.

Mother was appalled! She told Melvin that she didn't want to disappoint Dora, but she thought she'd agreed to something quite different. She was willing to make the exchange she thought she'd agreed to, and she'd pay for the survey, but she couldn't sign the agreement as it stood.

Melvin said if she didn't sign the deed the way he'd drawn it up, he'd stop guarding our land when we weren't there, and he couldn't guarantee what would happen then.

When Mother refused, Melvin said his brother should never have sold us the land in the first place, and stormed off. That winter, he planted a row of pines across the path from our property to Wilderness Way.

Mother looked at the row of young trees and shook her head. How could there be such a terrible misunderstanding between old friends?

Then Dora died.

Mother sent a note of condolence. Melvin answered with a repeated demand for the land.

"So much for Dora's house," said Daddy.

"But, William, what will we do when we need help with the property?"

"We'll manage."

◆   ◆   ◆

The solution to Mother's problem came with a new neighbor on Catfish. His name was Mark Browne.

The south end of our Catfish Lake shoreline is on a half-moon shaped cove, of which we own about half.

The other half was owned by Melvin Snyder.

In the Depression, Melvin offered to sell Mother his half for a hundred dollars, but we didn't have a hundred dollars.

Melvin sold the land to Mark Browne.

Before Mark came, the cove was one of my favorite places. Deer lived there. Delicious wild blueberries grew beside the shore, and there was a little swamp where cattails grew. One summer, I discovered a flexible sapling. If I pulled it down and held on to the right part of the trunk, I could jump up and the little tree would swing me across the soggy ground and deposit me on the other side, just like Tarzan!

At the far side of the bay, was a pond with clear water and water lilies, and you could sit on a log and watch the minnows and tadpoles, then take home a water lily or two and put them in the green pitcher on the kitchen table.

I'd gained a couple of inches the year Mark arrived, and the flexible little sapling had became a tree, so I didn't feel so bad when Mark filled the marsh and began building a house for himself, his wife, and their son.

Mark was an easy-going man with a weathered face and a drawling voice. I remember him as wearing stained overalls with a broken strap. Marjorie and I used to call him "And That There" because that was how he ended most of his sentences. Mother said we shouldn't make fun of other people's speech. She said Mark was a "diamond in the rough."

Mark got a license as a fishing and hunting guide, and he built a couple of tourist cabins to rent. In the winter, he hired out as a builder.

Mark did odd jobs for Mother. They had a few friendly misunderstandings. Nothing as bad as Melvin, of course. Just minor irritations.

For example, simple as our cottage aspired to be, Mother, tried to keep some aesthetic standards, a fact that Mark did not comprehend. He specialized in rustic. That crossed plank door to the bathroom was Mark's. Mother hated that door, but she didn't want to hurt Mark's feelings, so it stayed. Now it's part of the ambiance.

One year, Mother noticed that the wooden flooring of the front porch was rotting, so she asked Mark to build us a new porch floor.

That winter, Mark worked on a job that required a lot of concrete. He proudly told Mother how, when the contractor mixed more than was needed, he got the excess cheap. That's why the floor of our once dainty front porch is now a massive block of rough-poured concrete.

Mark's the one who installed the fake maple plasterboard over the studs in the big room.

I was of two minds about that plasterboard. It looked all right, but it covered up my poem. I had written a poem about the woods and the lake, and how they made me feel. It won the freshman literary contest in Southwest High School. I made a copy of it in my best artistic printing, and thumb-tacked it on the wall beside the kitchen door. When the plasterboard went up, I asked Mother to leave it there, the way people leave treasured things in graves. It's probably still there, if the mice or the carpenter ants haven't eaten it.

Mother wanted to put insulation between the plasterboard and the outer siding, but Mark talked her out of it. He said that a layer of air between two surfaces was insulation enough. That was how double-paned windows worked, and that there. Mother was too polite to argue.

Mark didn't have much use for our cottage. He said that, to be honest, it wasn't worth working on. The snow would get to it some winter, or a storm would come along and it would just fall down. He said he'd be happy to build us a new one. Cheap.

He had a suggestion for our Meta Lake shore, too. It was a shame to let the place go to waste. What with Daddy and Mother so interested in religion, and that there, they could just give him the property and he'd build a church camp where kids could swim, and walk in the woods, and get to know God, and that there.

Mother thanked him but said she really liked Meta Lake, and she didn't think many Vilas County children were deprived of exposure to lakes and trees.

Mark may not have agreed with Mother's views on interior decoration, but he totally sympathized on the subject of Melvin Snyder.

Mark hated him.

When Melvin sold any of his property, he always kept a strip of bordering land. I don't know why. Most of the strips wern't big enough to build on.

The strip Melvin kept back from Mark was between Mark's land and the county road. Melvin never said a word about it until Mark finished his driveway. Then Melvin closed it off.

I wish we'd known earlier that it's illegal in Wisconsin to sell access-locked property!

Mark claims that after he took Melvin to court and won, Melvin started a vendetta. Mark said Melvin dumped garbage on his property and threw nails on his road.

Mark said it was Melvin who stole our hand pump from the little house on Meta. "He's got it set up on that plot of land he's trying to sell over by the channel. Go see for yourself."

We looked. On one side of the entrance to the Cranberry Channel, Kelly's Indian still gazed out over the lake. On the other side, set proudly on a spit of land, was a bright red water pump. Ours? Could be.

"That old man sure likes to make trouble," said Mark. He sucked on his cigarette, "And that there."

The spring after Daddy died, Mother got a letter from Melvin Snyder. He was planning a trip to California and wanted to stop in Kansas City and see her. Mother was relieved and happy. She and Melvin could be friends again.

Melvin walked in the door holding his old unsigned bill of sale. When Mother wouldn't sign it, he swore at her, walked out and slammed the door behind him.

Mother died a couple of weeks later. Her doctor blamed Melvin Snyder.

Mark stuck it out for a decade or two until the taxes got to him. He sold his cabins one by one, and then his house, and bought a Christmas tree farm down Evergreen Road.

Now there's a whole colony on Mark's half of the cove. The new people have "improved" Mark's old tourist cabins with built-on rooms and insulation and heating. They've filled in the rest of the swamp and put in sand beaches and grass. They have piers and boathouses and big inboard speedboats. Their cabins are winterized. I'll bet some of them even have air conditioning!

They're nice people. They keep an eye on our cottage during the winter. They can see it when the leaves are off the trees.

I'm grateful for summer leaves.

I'm grateful that I saw Jeff Snyder.

Melvin Snyder sold off almost all his property before he died. His children sold most of the rest.

Except for Jeff.

Jeff was the only Snyder who chose to stay year-round on the lakes. He built himself a small house on the Catfish shore. He never put in electricity. He used kerosene lamps and a wood stove.

Jeff took after his mother.

I'm sorry Jeff had to give up his place on the lake.

I'm grateful we still have ours.

Change

7

Change

It's ninety-four degrees outside.

I'm beginning to look forward to that air conditioner, even though Bob says it will probably shake the whole cottage. Maybe it'll shake out the carpenter ants. Rohaya, our cook in Indonesia, used to get rid of insects in flour and sugar by shaking the container. The little creatures couldn't leave fast enough. I learned not to ask the history of Rohaya's baked goods.

It's enervatingly hot! What if global warming is really happening? We can't air condition a whole planet! I wonder how much oil will be burned to get the energy just to run our air conditioner.

An oil company Bob used to work for keeps sending us literature about how global warming isn't proven. It must be hard to consider oneself as a possible cause of catastrophe. Like eating Rohaya's biscuits, it's easier to deny what would be painful to accept.

Deny it or not, change happens.

The train that Daddy used to ride from Chicago is long gone, and the tracks have disappeared. The old station is a tourist center.

Nowadays, we can start from California and drive on interstates almost all the way.

The first time I got on an airplane at the Rhinelander, Wisconsin, airport and arrived in New York the same day, it seemed like a miracle!

69

North Central Airlines had two airplanes then, both DC-3s. Their stewardess was the same girl who smiled from the picture on their brochure. Their logo, a mallard duck, was on the tail of both planes. You knew it was supposed to be a mallard because the place where a mallard has a white band around its neck wasn't painted in. The duck's head looked totally separate from its body. We used to say we flew on the "Decapitated Duck."

In time, our friendly little airline got bigger. It merged with other airlines. It went national. But it kept its logo.

When Bob and I lived in Malaysia, I had to come home for an emergency operation. I returned to Kuala Lumpur via Chicago and Tokyo. My carrier was Northwest Airlines. The tail of the huge airliner sported a mallard with the old familiar disconnect. I took my first journey over the North Pole on the wings of The Decapitated Duck.

We've come home to the cottage from so many places: Evanston, Kansas City, New York, California, Malaysia, Indonesia, Australia, and before that, Korea and Japan. For years, the cottage was the only stateside home we had.

The little house by Meta was Mother's idea. When the canvas on the old army tent rotted away, my parents dismantled the flooring and the frame and carried them down to the Meta shore, where they set them up again. Daddy hammered on siding, put in windows and a front door, and covered the plank roof with tarpaper. We brought down our old kerosene lamps and kerosene stove and the old car icebox. We bought secondhand beds and a table and chairs. An outhouse and a well with a hand pump finished the project. We painted the little house white. We used it as a cabana for swimming, a guesthouse for overflow, and a place to stay when the cottage was rented.

The little house on Meta was the first home Chris saw after we adopted him.

We found Chris in Germany. He was three-and-a-half, a small blond waif in need of holding. Chris spoke no English, my German was rudimentary, and Bob knew no German at all.

What a terrifying experience it must have been for Chris! To be pulled out of the small country orphanage that had always been your home! Yanked around the world by two immense strangers who don't understand you, and don't make any sense when they try! Losing everything you know!

The head of the orphanage told us to make it a complete break. New parents, new clothes, new toys, new language. Nothing should remind him of what he'd been for his whole life.

We disobeyed, of course.

We visited my sister in New York who had studied in Germany. We visited friends who spoke German. We homed in on Mother's German. I began to remember German phrases I didn't know I knew. Chris began to laugh.

Bob was still on leave, and we didn't yet have a stateside residence, so we took Chris to Eagle River. The cottage was rented the week we arrived, so we went to the little house. It hadn't been used for some time, but we thought nothing of that.

It was almost dark when we turned off the road. Twigs crunched under our wheels, and saplings slapped on the windshield as we jolted down the uncleared trail. We stopped in darkness. I unlocked the door, struck a match and lit a kerosene lamp, while Bob carried our little boy into the tiny room. Dim light flickered on the naked rafters and cobwebbed windows. The beds were stark and bare. A startled spider scurried across the floor.

I don't know what they'd told Chris in the orphanage. I don't know what he expected in America, but it certainly wasn't this!

He broke into tears.

The next day the renters left, and we moved into the cottage. We had supper on the porch, set a cozy fire in the fireplace and tucked Chris under the quilt on the box couch. The next day, he discovered the lake and the woods, and he laughed again.

Eventually, we had to take down the little house. After Melvin Snyder stopped watching out for it, things began to happen. Someone overturned the outhouse. Someone stole the pump. Someone shot out the window. Rain and snow got in and ruined the furniture. The floor began to rot. We were afraid kids might try to play in there, and the floor would break, and someone would get hurt. Bob had Mark Browne tear it down. Now the only thing left is a small pile of asphalt roofing that's illegal to throw in the swamp.

We were living in New York and cleared for another adoption, when Tim came along and surprised us. That summer, we bought a folding crib-playpen that fit in the back of our station wagon, and we all drove to Wisconsin.

We took the interstate to Chicago. New highways sped us past the northern suburbs and Milwaukee, but I missed the park at Fon du Lac and the river at Oshkosh. We picked up old Highway 45 at Appleton, and Bob and I began calling off familiar names: Wittenburg, Eland, Birnamwood…Antigo, Three Lakes, Clearwater…Home.

Chris joined in. Tim helped.

We've still got the baby gate we put in that summer. I'm told that it's too dangerous for children. They could get their heads caught. But it's handy for dogs.

The town has grown. Some of the old stores are empty. The old bank across from the old railroad station is a souvenir store, and the old five-and-dime is a shirt store. The candy store is still in its old place, but the post office has moved to the main street.

The secondhand store that was in the alley behind the clothing store has closed, and there is a new store where the co-op grocery store used to be. It claims to be a secondhand store, but its prices are too high. Most secondhand stores have become antique stores, and the remaining secondhand stores specialize. The one on Railroad Street features secondhand guns and camping equipment, and the one where the co-op used to be takes dishes and furniture on consignment. You seldom find useful things like ironing boards or plumbing parts, and if you do, they're priced like antiques.

Most of the fixtures at our cottage were put in during the Depression, when frugality was not only a virtue but a necessity. They were all bought secondhand, which may be why the faucets in the bathroom don't match, and why we can't replace the ones in the kitchen. The kitchen sink is an old model, and you can't get faucets that match the holes in the back. If we wanted to put in a new sink, we'd have to pull out the old one, and if we did that, we'd have to pull out the shelf beside the sink because that was built around it. And Bob worries about the pipes underneath. He's afraid that, as the cottage has settled, the pipes have taken some of the weight, and if we move them, the kitchen floor might fall. The cottage is a structural ecosystem. If you move one thing, it affects everything.

As the hill settles, so does the cottage. Every few years, Daddy used to drag a big house jack through the crawl space under the main room, crank up the floor, and shim things back to level.

A few years ago, Bob bought four secondhand jacks and left them in place. All he has to do is crawl in every couple of years and give them a few cranks.

The jacks hold up the main part of the cottage, but the kitchen, the bedroom and the back porch were built later and are a separate system.

One summer, Bob noticed that the post holding up the corner of the bedroom was listing badly. He got out a spade and started to dig a hole to find out what was wrong. After two digs, he encountered no resistance. A badger had burrowed a tunnel beside the post, eaten part of it, and built a nest. The post was just waiting to fall in. Bob filled the hole with concrete and reset the post. I worried about the badger, but Bob said there were worse things than being dispossessed.

Until recently, our appliances were all secondhand, which has something to do with why we had to build the bedroom wall around the refrigerator.

When I was little, there were heavy curtains between the bedroom and the kitchen. Curtains often served as walls. We still have the set that crosses the living room. There used to be another curtain that shielded the area around the fireplace. When it got cold, we put on sweaters, pulled the curtain, cuddled in blankets in front of the fire, and roasted sausages, toasted marshmallows, and popped corn.

We took that curtain down when we got an electric heater and a propane stove.

When the cottage was wired for electricity, Mother bought a secondhand refrigerator. The only place to put it was in the bedroom-kitchen opening. Then the curtain could only be pulled as far as the side of the refrigerator, and the refrigerator door just cleared the back door. The refrigerator coils were in the bedroom, and it was a noisy refrigerator.

Bob got tired of waking to the sound of a starting refrigerator, so he built a wall where the curtain used to be, put in a door, and constructed a neat little box around the refrigerator to muffle the sound. The box extended into the bedroom. The bedroom dresser just fit between it and the outside wall, and there was even a shelf over the box to store blankets.

A few years ago, that old refrigerator gave out. They don't make refrigerators like that any more, and for a while we thought we would have to build a new wall, but luckily a friendly dealer found an old model that was almost the right size. It was missing its egg tray, and the vegetable section kept falling off its rack, but Bob fixed the rack, and I found a makeshift tray. Now it fits right in.

Meanwhile our ski boat has become a "classic boat."

When the *William Alice* fell apart, we bought a secondhand aluminum fishing boat. The owner threw in a five horsepower outboard motor, all for only a hundred dollars.

Our aluminum boat was an entirely satisfactory fishing boat, but the motor was a disappointment. It seemed all right at first. It would chug smoothly out into the middle of the lake. Then it would stop. Dead. It didn't matter what you did. You could wear your arm off, and exercise your vocabulary to the limit. It wouldn't start. It wouldn't even cough. It was a one-show-a-day performer.

That winter someone stole it out of our boathouse. How we laughed!

We remained a rowboat family until the boys grew bigger and water skiing became important.

We rented *Terposh* at a marina in Eagle River. She had a fifty-five horsepower motor. She started with a key! She had a tough vinyl hull, an audacious horn and a light. And she was fast!

I can see Chris now, his hair blowing, his sun-tanned body glistening in the spray, as he jumped the wake and jumped back again. He skied on one ski. He tried no skis and almost stayed up. I can hear his triumphant laugh.

Of course, we bought the boat. We named her *Terposh*. "Ter" means "very" in Indonesian, and P.O.S.H. stands for "Port, Out; Starboard, Home" which, in the days of empire, denoted the finest shipboard accommodations on the way to and from the Far East.

Terposh exploded our horizons. For the first time, we could boat the length of the chain. We could travel through the lakes to Eagle River and pull up at the town dock. We could glide through the channel to Cranberry Lake, disembark at the dam to watch *Terposh* ride up the hoist, and then we could skim up to the Northernaire Hotel for lunch. We could sweep across Catfish Lake at sunset, dock at Everett's resort, have a candlelight dinner, and idle home under the stars.

And we could watch the houses going up around the lake. Big houses!

Bob viewed them with disdain.

"Those people don't want a place in the woods," he says. "They just want a lake in their front yard."

With the new houses, came new regulations.

You're no longer allowed to "improve" your shore. You can't fill in wetlands. You can't build a house any closer than seventy-five feet from the water. You can't build on less than a hundred and fifty feet of shoreline. You can't cut down a tree without a permit. And you have to pump out your septic tank.

The septic tank thing came as a shock!

We weren't sure where our septic tank was. The family lost track of it shortly after Mother had it installed. We only located it a few years ago when a rusty corner appeared near the propane tanks. When the County insisted we have our tank drained, we put in a whole new septic system so we'd know where to tell somebody to go to pump it out.

We never did find the end of the drainpipe from the kitchen sink. It's out in the woods somewhere.

When you are looking at ten acres of your own land, surrounded by acres and acres of other people's untenanted land, you tend to trust nature a lot. We used to pull unwanted trash down to the marsh beside Meta Lake where it obligingly sank among the cranberry bushes. We were never around in the winter, so we were unaware that segments of the larger pieces, old stoves for example, and the piano, reappeared when the leaves fell. Even that fact went largely unnoticed for a long time because, for a long time, no one wandered that way between October and April. We summer people were gone, and the winter residents moved back into town before the snows came because the roads weren't cleared.

We were better housekeepers nearer to the cottage. We threw lime into our privy, kept its holes covered, and buried our garbage. Every year, we went a little farther down the garbage path to dig the deep hole into which we deposited empty cans and bottles. We covered every deposit with a little dirt. At the end of the summer, we filled the rest of the hole with dirt and covered it over with leaves.

The goal was to dig a hole deep enough to handle a season's worth of garbage, and still leave adequate depth to seal it in the fall.

Many years passed before erosion uncovered those caches of rusty tin and collectible glass, and we learned to handle nature like fine china.

Erosion isn't to blame for everything. Erosion didn't wipe out all those little frogs and fish eggs. Our marshes are getting drier, and there's something wrong with the woods.

About fifteen years ago, the birches began dying. Some kind of bug, people said. The forest used to gleam with rising columns of white. Now, most of the birches lie fallen, pale scars over softening centers. A few scrawny saplings bear a few limp leaves, and a few dead titans still stand, gaunt and headless reminders of former grace.

It happened before. When I was a little girl, the birches died, and Mother cried. Then new birches grew amid the maples and the poplars, and the woods gleamed white again.

Now we've got gypsy moths. They attack the poplars and the aspens. The canopy is thinning. You can see pitiful lace-cut leaves way up there. Grass grows on the forest floor where there never used to be enough light.

But there are new maple seedlings coming up, and oak and evergreen. Maybe there'll be a new kind of forest! A new place for children to explore!

Last year, we found a hollow log beside the upper path. It was covered with deep scratches. Was the bear just sharpening his claws, or was he looking for honey?

There's a place down by the shore where beavers have built a twig-entwined home. They gnawed down a couple of trees and built their house right on the water. They never got a permit, either!

Sometimes you find a feather on the path. You can hold it and stroke it and imagine how it had felt to be way up there, its vanes quivering in the wind.

And there are stones.

The glaciers ground over all kinds of terrain and made all kinds of geological history. You find it in the stones. Big ones, half buried in the woods. Little ones beside the shore. A glint of quartz along the path. The gleam of dark green striated with brown and grey. A clear sandwich of mica. The deep, velvet black of wet basalt. History liquefied by fire, and rounded by wind and water.

Children pick up stones and put them in jars with water and admire them, until it's time to put them back on the earth where they belong.

There are lots of things to discover.

The first time Chris went exploring all by himself, he came back with two girls.

We used to think that Chris would be the one to watch over the cottage, but his wife hated the place. I don't know why. Maybe she wanted vacations with room service.

It makes you wonder why you love a place. Is it the place, or is it the memories? Is it both?

Love makes magic in places. I remember introducing Bob to the lakes and the woods, and to my childhood secrets. I remember making love in front of the fire. I remember how, over the years, Bob made the cottage a part of himself with planning and work and love.

We held our breaths the first time Tim took his Kristi, to the cottage.

Kristi is a California girl, and California's beauty is formidable. Its great mountains and rugged shoreline and towering redwoods make you feel like you should be climbing up a rock face with a backpack full of water bottles and beef jerky.

Northern Wisconsin suggests that you cast for musky or swim across a lake, but at the same time, it whispers that you might lie back in the boat with your hand trailing in the water, or lean against your love and watch the sunlight in the trees.

Tim called us from town the morning after he and Kristi arrived. "How did she like it?"

"She got out of the car, looked around, and said, 'This is paradise!'"

Thank you, Lord!

Other Moccasins

8

Other Moccasins

The air conditioner is in! It doesn't look as bad as I feared, and it doesn't shake the whole cottage as Bob feared. For a while, we were both afraid it wasn't working. It took a couple of hours to make much of a difference. Bob says that was because it had so much to do. The whole area above the rafters must have been like an oven on broil! At any rate, the air conditioner is here now, and working, and we're cool, and I'm feeling much better.

Outside, it's in the nineties, and probably dangerous for me.

So here I am, a prisoner in air conditioning.

I look around.

Above my writing table, hangs the mounted head of a wild boar that Bob shot in Sumatra about fifty years ago. In its mouth, it holds a peacock feather (a gift from some friends who had a peacock) and an American flag from some past Fourth of July.

And there's that mandala on the wall above the couch. Funny that a Native American ceremonial shield and a South African independence leader should have almost the same name.

The hand-woven couch cover from India was a gift to Mother when she was active in the Women's Foreign Missionary Society. Mother was a big fan of Mahatma Gandhi, who was a big fan of weaving cloth to establish independence from Britain, and probably from foreign missionaries, as well.

No matter how well-meaning a conqueror may be, there's always somebody like Gandhi or Mandela to muddy the waters.

Our American forebears went from being conquerors to being conquerees, to being independent citizens. That is, most of them did. It depends on your forebears.

Before the English set foot in Virginia or New England, a group of Iroquois Chippewa Indians migrated from somewhere on the Atlantic coast to the area around Lac du Flambeau, Wisconsin. Tradition says they were looking for better hunting and fishing, but chances are they were forced out by the Algonquin. At that time, this Wisconsin lake country was occupied by the Lakota Sioux. The Chippewa forced the Sioux to move farther west, where they had to give up fishing and learn to hunt buffalo.

The Chippewa didn't call their new home "Lac du Flambeau." That name was given to one of their lakes by the French fur traders, who were the first Europeans to exploit this area. It is the French translation of a Chippewa phrase meaning "Lake of the Torches." The Chippewa liked to spearfish at night by the light of the torches they carried in their birch-bark canoes.

In due time, the Chippewa, like most native Americans, were forced onto reservations, where they were given tax-free autonomy and encouraged to stop hunting and start farming.

This probably sounded good to well-meaning, hardworking, underpaid employees of the Bureau of Indian Affairs, but the Lac du Flambeau Reservation is mostly woods and lakes and sand. Farming doesn't work.

The forest was a good resource until the first growth of hemlock, oak and pine was gone. Then the Lac du Flambeau Chippewa were in trouble. The Bureau of Indian Affairs tried to help. They knew that the Chippewa were fishermen, so they gave them a fish hatchery.

In Grandfather's day, the Chippewa still sold a little timber, but they mostly hunted, fished, gathered wild rice, and worked as handymen and filling station attendants. They also made a little money selling beaded belts and miniature birch-bark canoes, until the Japanese started making beaded belts and little canoes and undersold them.

When I was little, the Lac du Flambeau Chippewa seemed to have given up their heritage. I was disappointed that they didn't go around in feathers and beads and moccasins, but wore overalls and boots like everybody else. I guess they'd learned that looking and acting like an Indian had its disadvantages.

Their odds got better when some Native American student volunteers came up from the Southwest to re-acquaint the Chippewa with their tribal traditions.

By the time our kids were little, the Chippewa were having powwows on Tuesdays and Thursdays, and the public was invited.

The powwow setting was lovely, with the woods and the lake. We sat on bleachers watching befeathered college students leaping about a campfire, accompanied by a shuffling group of embarrassed locals, while three men in beaded shirts and headdresses hammered on a drum. Before passing the hat, the master of ceremonies invited everybody to join in. The kids loved it, leaping and shuffling with the best.

One problem with educating people about their history and traditions is that they begin demanding their rights. The Chippewa had rights to fish the lakes.

Fishing is a big thing up here, and not just for Indians. Fishing means tourists, and tourists are the lifeblood of an area where the soil is mostly sand, the old trees are mostly gone, and there isn't much industry. Fishing brought my Grandfather up here. We wouldn't be here if it weren't for fishing.

When I was little, I used to watch swarms of minnows darting around under our dock. Clumps of translucent fish eggs floated here and there. If a tree fell into the water, we left it there because it attracted fish. You could see black bass nudging the waterlogged trunk. When Daddy took out the boat before dawn, we could count on fish for breakfast.

As the people population increased, the fish population went down. The government started stocking the lake, putting in baby fish in the spring, so that tourists could take out mature fish in the summer.

Time passed. There were limits as to the size and weight of the fish you were allowed to keep.

More time passed. You weren't allowed to keep some kinds of fish at all. You had to throw the poor mouth-torn animals back for someone else to hook.

The Chippewa refused to cooperate. They said their original land treaties gave them unlimited fishing rights.

If you think people get excited about embryos, try fish!

Local landowners were incensed! Their government had stocked the lakes. Who owned the stocked fish, the Chippewa or the U.S. taxpayer?

The Chippewa had an answer. Their hatchery put thirty million baby fish in the lakes every year. They were simply recouping their investment.

A closer look at the treaty seemed to allow a compromise. The Chippewa could fish as much as they liked, but only with spears. And maybe torches. Tourists would like torches.

The Chippewa sharpened their spears and bought floodlights. Bass love floodlights! The Chippewa were spearing fish by the thousands.

Taxpayers don't take things like that lying down! Soon the Chippewa had to run a gauntlet of angry protesters just to get to their boats. The media loved it!

That was a few years ago.

It's calmed down now, although a woman complained to me the other day that there's a lake in the northwest of the county that is completely fishless because of the Chippewa.

Apocryphal?

Maybe.

I don't know how I feel about the Chippewa and floodlights and fish.

I owe both sides. I owe my grandfather, who built this place, and I owe the Indian who helped him.

Remember that slot machine at the old Clearwater store?

I played that machine. Once. One summer, I saved a nickel and kept it in my shorts pocket all the way from Evanston. Then, when Mother and Daddy were busy at the back of the store, and Marjorie had gone out to the privy, I put my nickel in the slot and pulled the handle. It made an awful noise! Those oranges and lemons and apples clanked around like nobody's business! I looked to see if

Mother had heard. She had. She was shaking her head. I looked back at the machine. It showed two lemons and an orange. No money in the cup.

"Have you learned anything?" Mother was beside me.

"I guess so."

A couple of years later the slot machine disappeared. Wisconsin had banned gambling.

I remember that slot machine with affection.

I remember it particularly now, when I see the flashy new billboards. "Lake of the Flames Casino! Blackjack! Poker! Unlimited slots!"

And I smile.

Storms

9

Storms

The heat has broken! There's a breeze. It smells like rain.

I'm sitting on the back porch with a book open on my lap. Bob is below, making something. I don't know what yet. The whole cottage is a palette for his carpentry.

It's getting darker. A raindrop taps the porch roof, then another.

The basement door creaks and thuds shut.

The wind rises. Branches dance. The rain increases to a torrent.

Bob comes up the porch steps. He is sopping. He grabs a swimming towel and rubs himself off.

"Wet?"

He grins. "An understatement." He puts the towel around his shoulders and sits down to enjoy the storm.

Below us, the lake is covered with dancing white.

"Good that you covered the boat."

Terposh, buttoned under her canvas overcoat, is bucking against the bumpers on the dock.

"Came up fast, didn't it? Hope they got all the camp kids in."

It can be scary out on the lake in a wind storm, particularly in a rowboat. It's hard to keep the prow into the froth-topped waves when they're doing their best to roll you sideways. Sometimes, if the rain is heavy, you can't see where you're going. But you know that you have to get to shore because of the lightning. Lightning strikes the highest thing around, and a child in a rowboat on top of a big wave can be the highest thing on a lake.

A flash of lightning. I count. One. Two. Three. There's a roll of thunder.

"Still a ways away."

Lightning is unlikely to strike our cottage. The surrounding forest trees are too tall. But you can't tell. Wisconsin storms speak in many languages.

A couple of years ago, a tornado took out all the old pines between my friend Kathy's house and the lake. Last year, a tree fell on our van and crushed the bubble top. If a big tree fell on the cottage, it would go down like a bunch of matchsticks.

This storm is going to be a good one! We hear trees cracking down in the forest. So far, none have fallen on the house.

As a child, I loved storms, rolling thunder, stinging flashes of lightning, and rain pouring down as though practicing for Noah's flood.

Storms were exciting for lots of reasons. For example, Grandfather forgot to put a damper in the chimney, so when it rains, the raindrops thwack right down into the ashes.

Grandfather also neglected to put a protective layer between the planks of the ceiling and the rolled asphalt that comprised the roof.

We've corrected that now, but when I was little, I spent a lot of time lying on the box couch, looking up at the ceiling and wondering.

At the peak of the ceiling there was a hole about six inches in diameter. Above it, rose a little metal cylinder topped with its own little peaked roof.

Why was it there? Was to let out kerosene fumes? Was it for ventilation? Had Grandfather borrowed an architectural practice from the Middle East? Had Bedouins used such openings in their tents to vent the heat of the desert?

One thing I was pretty sure of. Heat rises, and cold falls. Hot air going up was fine when the weather was warm, but in chilly weather that hole in the center of the ceiling allowed heat from the fireplace to escape, while the cold air from outside fell down on us.

I thought, too, that our bat might live up there. He tended to appear after sundown and swoop around the room, while Daddy laughed and Mother put her arms up and gasped warnings to be careful that he didn't get tangled in our hair. I wonder what happened to our bat.

When I lay on the box couch and gazed at the roof, I saw something else, too. Little pinpoints of light. I knew what they were. It didn't matter how much Daddy crawled around on the roof with a brush and a pail of hot pitch. The roof just kept leaking.

We had flashlights by our bedsides, and raincoats, and handy umbrellas. There were chamber pots under the beds so we wouldn't have to go to the outhouse in the rain.

But we had holes in our roof.

When I think of the storms of my childhood, I remember myself on the box couch, cuddling under warm sheets and soft quilts, while nature tore around outside. First came the thunder and the lightning and the wind. Then came the cozy rumble of rain on the roof. Then came the soft plop of water on the floor.

Then came Mother's voice. "Get the pans!"

Up we sprang! Out came the flashlights, and out came the buckets; the two galvanized pails from the back porch, the cooking pans from their hooks above the oil stove, the soup kettle, the little blue enamel berrying pail, each container with its own sonic frequency. We scurried about the cottage, flashlights in hand, examining the floor for wet spots. Big wet spots got big pans. Little wet spots got little pans. The plops of water on wood gave way to the pings of water on metal. We knew where most of the leaks were. It didn't take us too long to set our containers and crawl back into the warmth of our beds.

Ting, pang, splat, tick…Each pan played its own unique part. Each had its own timbre, frequency, and rhythm that constantly changed as the volume of water in the containers increased.

I sank back into sleep to a percussion lullaby.

Rights of the Heart

10

Rights of the Heart

Look!

The sun is shining, but it's not hot!

The air conditioner is silent. You can hear the leaves.

I've opened all the windows and doors, and a breeze sweeps through the whole cottage, bringing the scent of pines and water.

I'm on the back porch with my laptop.

This isn't the original back porch, the one with the shelf and the tubs of water. That porch got so rickety that we had to replace it. Our new porch is bigger and has a sink with running water, but its construction is essentially the same. Studs support a ceiling of planks and rafters. The floor has spaces for water to drain through.

There've been a couple of other changes. We have a turnaround at the top of the driveway so you don't have to back up to get out, and the new screen door opens in.

That makes a lot of difference because there's no landing on the top of the back porch steps. When the screen door opened out, you had to lean back and duck to one side to give it room. Carrying groceries up to the back porch was almost impossible.

You can push the new door open from the steps, and put your parcels on the table while you unlock the kitchen door and kick over the stone that holds it in place.

Now everybody uses the back door, and the front porch holds a pile of firewood.

◆   ◆   ◆

A family of phoebes favors the trees beyond the back porch. I think they have a nest somewhere above the cottage because every once in a while, one of them will drop straight down past the porch and, in a second or so, pop back up again like an avian bungee jumper. They talk to each other and play a game of round robin. I've been trying to figure out the rules. They have three bases on the branches of three trees, and there is a bird on each. Every once in a while, one bird leaves a base and another bird takes its place. Then another bird leaves another base, and still another bird takes its place. I can't tell the birds apart well enough to tell which bird takes which place, and in what order, but I know that the same bird doesn't go back to the same base because I've seen new birds arrive while departing birds are still in view.

The birds wait their turns, alert, twitching their tails, and making excited little chirps. How much of their noise is impulse, and how much is communication? Birds would have a lot to talk about. They know so much about seeds and insects, and wind and light and stars.

There's an eagle that likes to perch on top of the old dead poplar down by the boathouse. You can tell when he is circling because the whole forest goes still.

There are crows, of course, and the occasional jay. We hear loons laughing at twilight, and a whippoorwill's lonely cry.

One fall, we boated through the channel when the ducks were gathering for their migration. There were hundreds of them resting on the water, glistening brown and green and white, conversing in soft, throaty sounds. We cut the motor back and moved slowly through them. They parted for us, lazily, saving every mite of energy for their long journey south. The next day, they were gone.

How many generations of loons have called from the lake, and how many generations of phoebes have nested in our eaves? We're into the fifth generation, ourselves.

It's been a long time.

I was six the winter that Grandmother died. I don't remember much about it except that I was expected to be heartbroken. I was mostly curious. I'd never seen a dead person before. I was disappointed that it just looked like Grandmother with make-up. Grief came later, when I called and no one was there.

Every summer during the Depression, the cottage was full. People came from everywhere, cousins, nephews and nieces, their friends and their children. Nobody had any money, so we depended on each other for holiday escapes. The cottage expanded like an accordion. One week, we slept twelve people: two in the bedroom, two on each studio couch, one on the box couch, three on the floor, one on the back porch, and one child on the back seat of a car. Oh, yes, and two in the little house. Fourteen!

Then came the war and gas rationing. Fewer trips to the cottage. Fewer trips of any kind.

There were summers when we didn't get up at all. Mother hired a woman from Clearwater to clean the cottage for the renters, who still came up because they lived nearer and could spare the gas.

Mother didn't raise the rent, even though the cottage was costing more, and we used it less. She said that good renters are too valuable to risk losing. Besides, her renters were second generation. They had rights of the heart.

The war ended. The cottage came slowly back to life, but differently. Not as carefree. More deeply aware of enjoyment.

Mother and Daddy died within four months of each other. Daddy died in the fall. Mother stayed around long enough to hold my newborn son before she joined him in the spring.

Marjorie and I were left with the cottage, the renters, and the taxes.

We couldn't understand why our taxes went up so much when we made no improvements on the property. Bob investigated and found that taxes are based on shoreline. Every time someone sold a piece of shoreline, the assessment was adjusted to what that property had sold for. The economy was growing. The old wandering woods was shrinking. People were making investments in shoreline properties. Assessments kept going up .

We went to the town council. We pointed out that we had made no improvements on our property, and, although we owned shoreline on two lakes, a lot of it was cranberry bog, or too low to meet septic requirements, or too steep to build on. It couldn't be worth much.

The council was sympathetic. They sent out an appraiser. He agreed that much of our shoreline belonged in a lower tax bracket, but another part had been under-appraised. Our taxes remained the same.

We wondered if we should sell some property.

The trail to the schoolteacher's house was now a driveway for several families who had bought and built on Melvin's old land.

We owned some wandering woods down that way. If we sold a piece, we'd have less shoreline to be taxed.

The lot sold for enough money to raise our next assessment. Our taxes went up. We ended where we started, but without the lot.

By that time, the renters had distilled into two families, the Pruits and the Ketwingers. They were keepsakes like the organ and the box couch. Their grandparents had rented from our grandparents and their parents had rented from Mother. We never saw them. They sent us letters saying when they would be coming to the cottage, and they sent checks when they left. The Pruits didn't pay as much rent as the Ketwingers because, after Mother's cleaning woman died, the Pruits opened the cottage, cleaned it, and treated it as their own, donating linens and dishes and little objects of art.

The Ketwingers treated the cottage as their own, too, in their own way. Every year we cleared their empty bottles from the yard.

We knew our tenants were paying about half the going rate.

We raised the rent.

The Ketwingers disappeared into Montana.

The Pruits wrote that they had been wondering for a long time why we charged them so little. They were happy to keep opening the cottage and leaving us little mementos, until Mr. Pruit died, and Mrs. Pruit went into a retirement home. For several years, we exchanged Christmas cards. Hers grew progressively smaller and more pious, and eventually faded away entirely.

Years went by, and more people earned rights of the heart.

Bob's mother loved the cottage. I think it reminded her of her Oklahoma childhood. She crafted a rack to put beside the hearth for firewood. She contributed her old cast-iron waffle iron and some cake pans, and she rocked our children in the old rocking chair. She spent one whole winter making a quilt for the box couch. You can't buy bedding that size, but Mom's quilt fits perfectly; squares of blue and green and brown and gold. It belongs.

Julie's marriage fell apart after World War II and she lost custody of her children. She could only have them a couple of weeks a year, so in June, no matter who was in the big cottage, the little house belonged to Julie. Her children wandered the paths where we had picked blueberries, and learned to swim where we had netted minnows.

Julie's son brought his bride to the cottage for their honeymoon. Not all rights of the heart come easily.

Marjorie was on vacation in the Middle East, and I was in my kitchen in Dobbs Ferry, New York, when the phone rang. My sister's voice was soft and distant, and terribly controlled. "Pat? Sam's had a stroke."

As soon as it was possible, Marjorie shepherded her wounded husband and two bewildered sons back across the ocean. When I saw Sam, I tried to hide my shock. Was this the confident man with the big laugh that my sister had married? He looked up from his wheelchair, forced a few strange sounds from a contorted mouth, and extended a twisted arm. His strong surgeon's hand had distorted into a trembling arc. I think he was trying to smile. I took the hand and tried to smile back.

"Welcome home."

Spring came, and I got a call.

"Are you planning to be at the cottage in July?" my sister asked.

"No. Why?"

"I want to take Sam."

She heard my gasp.

"I know it sounds crazy."

I regained my voice. "You're right. It sounds crazy. He can't walk. He can't talk. How will you manage?"

"I'll manage. The boys can help."

I thought of her irrepressible children. Oh, dear!

"Sam loves it there." Marjorie said. "I know he can't walk or talk, but he can see and hear and feel."

Every summer from then until Sam ran out of life, Marjorie loaded his wheelchair into the back of the car and drove him and her sons from New York to Wisconsin so her husband could enjoy his few fading senses in a place that he loved.

Marjorie was building a new life for herself when my turn came.

We were at the cottage. August was almost over, when Bob complained of a stomach ache. He took an antacid, but it didn't help.

I suggested he see a doctor, but Bob hated to admit to illness. He suffered for two days before he would go to the hospital.

The Eagle River doctor said it might be appendicitis. He sent us down to the Rhinelander Hospital where they had a surgical team. I knew that appendicitis, though not something to be taken lightly, is considered routine. But there was something about the doctor's voice that made me apprehensive.

The Rhinelander surgeon insisted they operate immediately.

What was the diagnosis?

He said he wasn't certain, and it would be at least an hour before we would get a report.

It was a lot longer than an hour before the surgeon reappeared.

Bob's tumor had been about to metastasize when they cut it out, along with much of his digestive system. He had a forty percent chance of pulling through the next five days.

We were allowed to see him, pale and still under a canopy of bags and plastic tubes.

"Most of that's antibiotics." the nurse reassured us. "Because there wasn't time for a proper prep."

We waited until Bob woke, pressed my hand, then slept again. Tim and I drove back through an empty evening to an empty cottage.

Tim did a lot of swimming and chopping wood that next week, while I spent a lot of time sitting on the back porch with the lake and the trees and the sun and the storms, wondering if I could get along without Bob.

Day by slow day, we waited until Bob was out of danger.

When Bob was released from the hospital, we took him to a motel where they had amenities like heat and air conditioning and food. He didn't like it. He wanted to go home.

The double bed in the bedroom was too high for him, so I put him on the bed between the organ and the bedroom wall. I slept on the box couch. Tim got the bedroom.

A week passed. Tim had to get back to school. Bob assured me he would be all right while I drove Tim to the airport.

It turned cold. The thermometer on the back porch read twenty-eight degrees. Fire-warmed air rose to the peak of the roof and rolled down its frost-chilled sides. Only a layer of half-inch plasterboard, four inches of stud space, and a wall of uncaulked siding stood between my precious invalid and the rising wind.

I pulled the window curtains. I put a blanket over the front door. I closed the door to the bedroom and turned on the oven. I fed the fire. I turned on two space heaters, one beside Bob's bed and one on my side of the room. I unplugged all unnecessary electrical appliances and prayed I wouldn't blow a fuse. The fuses held, and the cold spell broke before the pipes froze.

Bob could sit up and spend a little time in a rocker by the fire.

The maples turned. The forest glowed with red and orange and gold.

Bob could walk with a stick.

Snow sugared the clearing.

Bob was strong enough to travel.

"I knew I wouldn't die," he told me later.

"Maybe so," I replied, "but you sure know how to scare somebody!"

◆   ◆   ◆

Look! There's a doe in the clearing, with two little fawns. She raises her head. She sees me. For a moment, we share existence. She accepts and dismisses me. With dainty dignity, she steps into the forest, followed by one fawn. The other is eating. He looks up. Oh! A nervous look around, and in two bounds, he, too, is gone.

I think they sleep down in the hollow by the cove.

There are too many deer. The forest can't sustain them. They eat everything, brush, bark, and the shoots of new trees. They are an ecological menace, and there will be an open hunting season this year. It could be a question of starving or getting shot. So keep your heads down, little family. The property is posted, and there should be enough food to keep you, but beware of strangers of either species.

◆   ◆   ◆

I don't know why Mother left us the cottage as "joint tenants." If either Marjorie or I died, the entire property would go to the other with no regard for the rights of our children. We changed the deed to read "tenants in common." This protected the children, but discouraged either of us from making any changes.

I've had plans for the property ever since I was a little girl. When I was in grade school, I wanted to use it as a movie set for Longfellow's poem "Hiawatha." In high school, I visualized a theatrical stock company in a clearing over by Meta Lake. In college, I designed a theme resort, and when Bob and I were overseas, we agreed that we needed a place to go in the winter.

We considered building a three-room cottage on Meta Lake, where the little house had been. Or maybe a bigger house above my secret rock, a haven built into the hill, burrowing into the protection of the earth like the old sod houses did. Bob read hardware catalogues and investigated road construction and water pumps, while I drew plans, and more plans.

In the end, nobody did anything. You don't make that kind of investment without clear title.

Marjorie and I had gifted interest in the property to our children until the inheritance tax changed. Then we reconsidered. We saw inherited property tear families apart. Who could use the place?

When? Who would maintain what? Who would pay? If our property was divided, would everyone own useless slivers of shoreline and would no-one be happy?

We convened a family conference.

It was the taxes that did it. More people wanted to use the cottage than wanted to help pay for it. Bob and I bought out Marjorie's family's interest, Tim bought out his brother's interest, and our title became clear.

Everyone with a right of the heart is still welcome, of course. The only difference is that they come for free.

◆   ◆   ◆

I glance at my laptop.

There's so much more to write about!

The day Bob found out there was nothing holding up the hearth.

Standing by the organ, playing Grandfather's violin.

The children in the cove, who thought witches lived in our cottage because they kept hearing weird violin music.

Taking our children to the frontier fort in back of the snowmobile racetrack, to watch local kids, dressed up like cowboys, stage fights for the tourists.

The riding stables that came and went on Evergreen Road, and the drive-in movie which was born and died in the field behind the farmhouse where we used to buy milk.

Sitting in the motionless boat on a windless night, looking up at a moonless sky and identifying constellations.

Tales yet to be told.

Stories yet to be lived.

But listen!
The forest is singing.
I close my laptop.

Closing Up

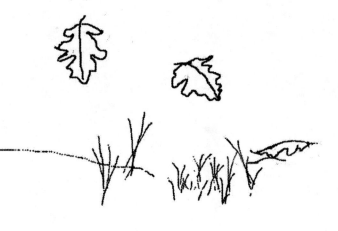

11

Closing Up

There's crispness in the air today.

I woke to the patter of feet on the roof. The chipmunks, the squirrels and the mice are impatient for the summer people to leave. A branch of the maple sapling beside the front door has turned bright tangerine. We had a fire in the fireplace last night.

It's time.

I'm always surprised by how quickly the seasons pass. It was only a few weeks ago that we were using our new air conditioner, and now autumn is coming. While we are gone, the earth will circle the sun, and this small familiar home will enter a place where I've never been. In all the ways that I know the cottage and the woods and the lakes and the sky, I've never been here in the winter.

I've seen pictures. Neighbors have sent them. I've seen snapshots of the brilliant fall foliage, and of the winter woods, leaf-bare except for evergreen pines and the spruce. I've seen pictures of the cottage, waiting, naked and alone, on an unfamiliar snow-drenched hill.

It doesn't seem many years ago that Bob and I were sitting on our hide-a-bed in Greenwich Village watching *This Is Your Life* on our first black and white TV.

The subject of the show was a valiant woman doctor who served people living in places almost impossible to reach in the wintertime, people who bunkered down in log cabins and dugout sod houses in an area where temperatures went down to forty below. There was a picture of her, dressed like an Eskimo, snowshoes strapped onto her boots, her doctor's bag on her back, grinning out from a coronet of fur.

"Look, Bob!" I exclaimed, "That looks like Meta Lake!" Turned out the woman lived in Eagle River.

Now the roads are cleared in the winter. We have neighbors who live here year round, and others who go south for the coldest months and come up for Thanksgiving and Christmas.

While we're gone, there will be a snowmobile festival in town. Eagle River is the Snowmobile Capital of the World! Snowmobiles come from all over to race. I wonder what Grandfather would say.

Tim and Kristi have been here in the winter. They couldn't stay in the cottage, of course. They stayed at a bed-and-breakfast over on Eagle Lake.

They rented a snowmobile and rode across frozen Catfish Lake. I didn't know snowmobiles have heated handles!

They described the ice castle that is built every winter in front of the old railroad station. They took pictures. It looks lovely!

Tim waded up through the snow to the cottage, took the key from the hidden place, and went inside. He has been in this room, seen all these dear familiar things, frozen and still. He retrieved a can of soup, which he and Kristi took back to their lodging and thawed for supper.

Tim and Kristi are talking about building a year-round house up here, a house set into the hill, with a foundation going down deep in the earth.

Wouldn't that be wonderful? The whole family could be up at the same time. We could stay later in the fall. Friends tell me the autumn colors reflected in the lakes are something you never forget.

Maybe some day I will touch the snow.

Tomorrow, we close the cottage for the winter.

That's easier than it used to be.

We don't have to board up the windows because we have new casements and better locks.

We don't have to take out the pier and pull the *William Alice* into the boathouse. We have a permanent pier, and we store *Terposh* at the marina.

I don't have to defrost the refrigerator with a hair-dryer.

We'll strip the beds and couches and put all the linens and quilts under plastic with mothballs, so our small, winter tenants don't use them for maternity wards.

We'll bring the porch furniture inside.

We'll drain the water system.

We'll make sure the windows are securely fastened.

We'll check that we have all the keys before we set the locks on the doors.

We'll turn off the lights.

Finale

12

Finale

The most glorious sunsets I've ever seen were in Sumatra. The winds from the northern and southern hemispheres meet at the equator and create every kind of cloud imaginable, piling one over another high into the sky. The setting sun through the moist tropical atmosphere splashes every color in the spectrum into this huge sweeping design. Breathtaking!

The next most beautiful sunsets I've ever seen are from the back porch of the cottage.

Our porch is high, level with the tops of the trees that grow down by the shore. You look right over the woods, over the two points of land that lie between us and the far shore of the lake. At the same time, you are sheltered by the trees around the cottage. They are forest trees, straight and tall. They are sparser now than they used to be, but you can see more of the water and more of the sky. We have two sunsets, one above the trees, one reflected in the water, separated by the darkness of the woods.

There is a time shortly before sunset when, if I'm busy in the house, Bob is likely to call me.

"Come out, Pat! It's almost here."

He's talking about the golden time, when the sun is just beginning to refract through the atmosphere, and the light on the tree trunks, always lovely in late afternoon, turns gold. Everything—earth, leaves, branches, the trunk of the trees—is gilded, just for a few minutes.

We sit down. The sun is so low that you can almost see the earth turn. It begins, a tinge of pink on the low edge of the clouds. It grows. We watch.

Clouds here sweep more from side to side than the billowing cumuli of the tropics. The colors feel softer, too. They glow more than they glisten. And they last longer, not like the sunsets in the tropics that seem to appear and disappear in minutes. Here, glory grows, spreads, sings for a long time before luminescence fades to grey-blue, lingering until the sky grows dark and filled with stars.

About the Author

Pat Maximoff's first published work appeared when she was five years old. It was a poem about a tree.

Since then, she has written and directed shows in Korea, Japan, Indonesia, and Malaysia; taught English literature in Sumatra; and helped found the International School in Kuala Lumpur. For two years, she was adjunct professor of theatrical production at the University of Malaysia.

She has been a stringer for *The Kansas City Star*, Australian correspondent for *Swimming World*, and an editor of *The Chamber Musician*. Her articles have appeared in *The Kansas City Star*, *The Singapore Straits Times*, and *The Sydney Morning Herald*.

Pat has a BS in Speech and Theater from Northwestern University.

When she isn't writing or teaching or directing, Pat plays the violin and coaches chamber music.

Through all of her busy life, Pat has retained a refuge in the Northern Wisconsin Woods. This sanctuary is the inspiration for *Rights of the Heart.*

978-0-595-38627-7
0-595-38627-X

Printed in the United States
54042LVS00004B/343-381